EAT, NAP, PLAY

How to Get Even More Out of
Your Child's Day for Less

ROBYN SPIZMAN AND EVELYN SACKS

Health Communications, Inc.
Deerfield Beach, Florida

www.hcibooks.com

Library of Congress Cataloging-in-Publication Data

Spizman, Robyn Freedman.
  Eat, nap, play : how to get even more out of your child's day for less /
  Robyn Spizman and Evelyn Sacks.
      p. cm.
    Includes index.
    ISBN-13: 978-0-7573-1361-5
    ISBN-10: 0-7573-1361-2
    1. Parent and child.   2. Child rearing.   3. Parenting.   I. Sacks, Evelyn.
  II. Title.
  HQ769.S653 2010
  649'.1—dc22

                                                              2009051558

Publisher: Health Communications, Inc.
          3201 S.W. 15th Street
          Deerfield Beach, FL 33442–8190

Cover design by Justin Rotkowtiz
Interior design and formatting by Lawna Patterson Oldfield

EAT, NAP, PLAY

The greatest job of all is being a mom.

This book is dedicated to the loving, hard-working,

multitasking moms of the world,

including our very own,

whom we treasure.

Contents

Acknowledgments

WE APPLAUD OUR EDITOR, Michele Matrisciani, who had a vision for this book and is one of the world's great new moms. Balancing authors, mommyhood, and more, she offered valuable perspective and insight. We deeply appreciate her bright ideas and warm ways.

To our literary agent, Meredith Bernstein, who continues to make things happen in the literary world with dedication and perseverance. Thank you for your guidance and support.

Special thanks to Robyn's husband, Willy, and The Spizman Agency, including Carly Felton and Shelley Kreimer, for their expert advice and assistance. Also, to the following individuals who contributed content to this book, we are grateful for your insights into raising kids and saving money:

Patty Brown
Bobbi Burger Brunoehler
Joseph Denton
Nancy and Wayne Freedman
Edie Fraser

Belinda Fuchs
Drs. Stephan and Marianne Garber
Donna Goldberg
Chris Heiska
Leslie Isenberg
Rachel Johnson
Tory Johnson
Kris Cain
Sheri Lapidus
Sharon Marshall Lockett
Annette Marcus
Amy Lynn McCarthy
Jaime Milner
Margaret Mix
Catherine O'Brien
Anne Rosenthal
Erica Salmon
Lori Simon
Pablo Solomon
Lynn and Wink Weinberg
Amy Zeide

From Robyn: This book is dedicated to my wonderful, beloved children (who still eat well and now work hard)—Justin (and his beautiful bride, Jaime) and our inspiring daughter, Ali, who all add meaning to my life and makes every day special and worthwhile. To my loving husband, Willy, who supports me at every turn around the clock, and to my amazing parents, Jack and Phyllis Freedman. Thanks to our extended family, and to Bettye Storne, our real-life angel. And, finally, much gratitude to our host of friends (way too numerous to mention but you all know you are!), especially talented teachers Lori Simon and Jaime Milner, who contributed wonderful information to this book, thank you one and all for making life sweet. And to my co-author, Evie, my deepest thanks. You wrote the book on how to be an amazing co-author and fantastic friend!

From Evie: This book is dedicated to my mom, Charlene Sacks, who has taught and supported me through every joy and challenge; to my dad, Arthur Sacks, whose love of language launched me and whose wisdom endures; to my children, Erica Sitkoff and Chuck Sitkoff, who are loving, self-reliant, and concerned for their world; and to my husband, Cary Rodin, loving supporter of my dreams and schemes, nonjudgmental and ever-present. . . . And to Robyn, friend in "words" and deeds.

Introduction

MOTHERHOOD IS CLEARLY THE BEST job in the world. Challenging, yes, but the satisfaction is beyond measure, the joy as huge as the effort. We wrote this book to share a wealth of ideas with you for making your life as a mom of toddlers to 'tweens even better. We want to inspire you to go beyond the eating, napping, and playing, and create a special and meaningful connection with your child. We're here to cheer you on!

As moms ourselves, we've been there—and are still doing that. Our kids have moved beyond morning naps and after-school snacks, and we've seen firsthand the incredible returns from our investment of time and love.

Who are we? Robyn is a mom, former teacher, media personality, founder of TheGiftionary.com, and best-selling author of many books on parenting. Evie is a mom, writer, and specialist in affordable fun. We're here to share our experiences and great ideas, but also to encourage you to find your special spark as a mom. We want you to feel confident, when you hit the pillow (exhausted) at night, that you've done your best for your kids and enjoyed the adventure.

So, how do you do it? How do you create a safe and healthy home, reasonable expectations, an appropriate sense of self-worth, and a lot of fun for your children? One thing we know for sure: You don't create it by buying more things. That happy, tired feeling at the end of the day (theirs *and* yours) comes from something else: a bond that grows from interacting in authentic, creative ways that are about spending time (as much as you have), not money.

Eat, Nap, Play is a book about the little things that make that time special. You won't find philosophies about child rearing in these pages. But you will find our ideas, as well as those of others, about getting something special out of every day—even days with meltdowns, lost math papers, and back-seat squabbles. It's about the fifty-cent craft that brightens a rainy day . . . the picnic on the grounds of the public library . . . the community book swap you organized . . . the time the kids took the dog to a nursing home to visit . . . the store-bought cake you turned into a treasure by decorating it with a cartoon character and a handful of broken candy.

As moms who have worked hard at parenting and seen great rewards, we know that the best things in life are not *things* at all. They are the time we spend, the skills we share, the example we set for our families. You picked up this book because you intuitively know this. But you want to do it just a little better than you might be able to do on your own. After all, you have a child now, and the stakes are high. We love that you want to make every day count, and we applaud your energy.

The pages that follow cover a lot of territory, like using technology to enhance family experiences, escaping the birthday party madness, and embracing swap and barter. Some of our subjects may be right up your alley; others may represent new ways of thinking. Our goal is that you enjoy the book and benefit from it wherever you are in your parenting adventure. We hope you have as much fun reading and using the book as we had writing it. We hope you try lots of our ideas and add your own special touches to make them your own.

Ultimately, we want to help you be the mom you want to be. A mom with a few more good ideas up her sleeve. A mom who isn't obsessed with perfection in herself or her kids. A mom who is resourceful, creative, and authentic in her parenting style. A mom who knows how to create fun and, when things get crazy, ask for help. A mom who longs for that feeling of satisfied exhaustion at day's end, knowing she spent time meaningfully with a deserving child. *A mom like you.*

Spend More Time and Less Money

CONGRATULATIONS ON JUMPING on board as we help you create a happier, less harried life with your family. Our goal is for you to discover more joy and meaning in each day, spending time with your kids in ways that really matter.

As moms, we know that when the focus is on spending time together, rather than money, the creative juices really start to flow. It's easy to spend money on our kids by stockpiling toys, gadgets, and the latest gizmo. But finding ways to enjoy being together without spending increases joy.

Who knew there were so many cash-free ways for kids to learn, grow, socialize, appreciate good food, enjoy technology, and become more independent and resilient? This book celebrates our philosophy, one that's been confirmed by happy moms (and kids) who have used our approach. It's rooted in this simple formula: spend twice as much time and half as much money.

The result is certainly money saved, but even more important, we raise children who know the value of a dollar and become more productive members of their families and communities. When special memories are made, not purchased, the entire family wins. There is simply no wiser investment in your children than time, your most precious commodity.

The Big Payoff

What's the return on this investment? Think happy mom, happy child, happy childhood. Smart, self-reliant kids who, before you know it, grow into self-reliant adults. Exposed to this way of thinking, children learn that, regardless of the circumstances they are faced with in life, they can be independent and see themselves as the solution. Recession? Job loss? They'll rise to any challenge without relying on money to experience the good stuff in life.

It's all about a new parenting attitude. Your pocketbook is not your boss. Regardless of income, job status, or the balance in your savings account, you can be the master of your money. This attitude will empower you to adopt and develop your own cost-free routines for your family. By teaching children that the lasting value is in the time we spend, not the money, we are teaching skills for a lifetime.

After all, as parents, we are our children's first and most important teachers. And the biggest lesson of all is that it's a better world when we can enjoy it on our own terms, less influenced by what's "spendy or trendy" and more by what really matters, like family, community, connection, and personal growth. We know you can make this change, and we're confident you're going to enjoy the ride. Welcome to a new and satisfying way of enjoying family time.

Keep It Simple

A more authentic, easygoing approach to life with kids starts with the universal wisdom that it's all about keeping it simple. It's about simple things you can do with your children to lighten the financial load while holding onto your priorities. We complicate things by thinking we need to have the latest and greatest thing. And whether you're a stay-at-home parent or out in the workforce, a life that's crowded with too many things, too many activities, and too much to manage leaves no room for the good stuff. When you simplify your parenting style and make parenting more affordable and less chaotic, family stress diminishes, and everybody benefits.

We know you are in the trenches, and we're here to offer support and insights. You'll build miles of smiles and happy memories every day as you become the mom you want to be.

Everybody hops on board at a different place in their lives. We've been doing this kind of parenting for years. You may be pretty practiced at it yourself, or possibly new to the mommy thing altogether. We welcome you all! As parents who have raised capable, engaged, community-minded kids who are making a difference in their careers and in life, we know it's a huge job to help them reach their goals. And we also learned, sometimes the hard way, that keeping things simple and focused never failed us.

Plain Smart Parenting

This approach to parenting is not only possible, it's just plain smart. And it doesn't mean living on barter, IOUs, or credit. We show you how to do more with less, but we're also realists. Our vision of a less money-dependent lifestyle does not mean a ban on spending for entertainment or satisfaction. It means just saying no to "everybody's doing it" or "everybody's buying it," and relying on your own creativity and innate parenting skills instead.

There are many things we want in life, but they shouldn't all have dollar signs in front of them. Like you, we value life's niceties. And when parents work hard, they reap great satisfaction from providing lovely clothing, meals, and educational opportunities for their families. But at the end of the day, living more money-free means embracing a lifestyle that is tasteful, not wasteful. It means enjoying the beauty of nature, counting our blessings, and focusing on what we have, more than on what we want.

Give a Skill, Change a Life

One of the most productive ways to spend time with your children is to share the best of yourself with them. Your kids know you as their parent, teacher, nurse, psychologist, playmate, provider, and arbiter of disputes. You also happen to be a person who's lived several decades and gotten good at quite a few things, thank you very much! Sharing these unique abilities with your children is a gift and a joy.

Begin by asking yourself what skills and talents you can share. We often underestimate the power of our talents because they come so easily to us. But to a child, a new, hard-earned skill is an exciting opportunity to gain and grow. Take bike riding, gardening, or just producing a long, lazy tone by pressing a fat piece of grass between your thumbs. Remember the pride you felt when you first wobbled down the street without training wheels or managed to shuffle a deck of cards? Skill-building is one of the most productive ways children grow. Become more conscious of what your children can learn through you. The following story is about a dad who did just that.

Thanks, Dad

Wayne is a father of two sons and a daughter. He is a fabulous pianist who decided that inspiring his kids to learn to play was something he wanted to do. Over the years, he made it a priority to always be available if his kids needed help with a particular piece. All three children were quite talented and, despite some grumbling about practicing, they kept at it over the years.

Wayne's wife, Nancy, observed, "Wayne's love of music inspired our children, and he continues to be such a great role model to them as they witness the true pleasure he still gets from playing the piano."

Their middle child, Scott, put his love of music and his talent to work to achieve an important goal. As a high school student, Scott had an opportunity to travel overseas as a volunteer. The program required that Scott come up with the cost of the plane ticket and spending money; a home stay and meals would be provided. So Scott got the brilliant idea to put on his own concert to raise the money. In addition to being a talented pianist, Scott is also very funny—the family's personal stand-up comic. Everyone who knew him knew his show would be entertaining.

The community theater space was donated, and everyone in the family helped Scott sell tickets, publicize the event, and handle many details. But Scott was in charge and brought down the house with a wonderful blend of comedic and musical talent. After he had taken his final bow, Scott thanked everyone who had made the event possible, including the owner of the theater, his siblings, and his many friends.

But his warm and conscious appreciation of Wayne was the sweetest moment of the evening. "And to my dad," said Scott as he took his final bow, "thanks for all those hours when we sat together at the piano bench. I learned so much more than the notes on the page."

Wayne was quiet but persistent in sharing his skill. It was never expected that any of the children would become a concert pianist, but he held onto his goal that they all would learn to play. All of Wayne's children acknowledge the gift and plan to share it with their kids one day. Sure, practicing was not always at the top of their list, but over time as they improved, they really enjoyed being able to play.

A Piece of Yourself

Whether it's the ability to play an instrument, dunk a basket, or roll a biscuit, we pass on a piece of ourselves when we take the time and patience to share these with our kids. Robyn's son and daughter, Justin and Ali, are great at arts and crafts. Their skill reflects the hours spent at the kitchen table with paper, paste, and paint. As a former art teacher, Robyn has an ability to turn trash into treasures, which she did, creating an art-filled home and experiences that could be enjoyed without expensive materials.

Evie has always been good with languages. When her kids were toddlers, she taught Erica and Chuck to speak and interpret those fun, made-up languages created by re-arranging sounds and syllables. Both became proficient at languages, and interested in the cultures and places behind them.

Yes, we all have talents and skills, whether we casually expose our kids or choose to consciously share what we know. How we entertain ourselves makes a bold statement to children. If they see us reading often and taking trips to the library, we are modeling behaviors that can spark intellectual curiosity and change a life.

Think about a skill you would like to teach your child or help him gain over time. Ask and answer these questions:

- What level of competence would you like him to achieve, and what will it take? If you're not able to share a particular skill you'd like your child to have, can you enlist a family member or close friend to be your skill-teaching proxy? What can you do for these people in return?
- At what age will you let your child decide if he or she wishes to continue with the learning?

Here are a few examples of skills you can share:

- Singing or playing a musical instrument
- Playing sports
- Doing handcrafts
- Speaking a foreign language
- Cooking and baking
- Painting, drawing, pottery, or other visual arts
- Home repair and DIY projects

Sharing skills can lead not only to competence, but to a habit of spending time together. We've found that kids who achieve some level of mastery at a young age are more confident and self-reliant. They value the fulfillment they receive from their special pursuits, which can mean they don't feel as much of a need for external gratification from costly gadgets and equipment—the trendy stuff that can be costly to provide and disappointing to see unused.

Consider these ways to encourage your child to get interested in a new skill:

- **WATCH AND LEARN.** When the child of a friend or neighbor is having a recital, swimming in a meet, or playing in a tennis match, take your child to watch. Seeing another child succeed can be a strong motivator. It's also a wonderful way to support families you care about as you expose your kids to a skill in action.

- **BRING IT TO KID SCALE.** A large piano might be overwhelming to someone barely able to stretch his arms, but a used electric keyboard may be a less intimidating way to start. Search for a child-size version of the instrument or tools needed to perform that sport or skill. Comb yard sales to find a set of junior golf clubs or short-handled cooking implements.

- **MAKE IT HANDS-ON.** Kids learn by doing. Ever notice in grocery stores with those tiny carts how much more content the kids are than the kids who are trailing behind the parent's cart? Prepare a small garden patch and let your daughter decide what to grow, plant the seeds or seedlings, and, of course, weed and water. Share those first crunchy cucumbers with family or friends. First fruits indeed!

Because Time Is Priceless

Of course, the *amount* of time we spend together matters. But just being there isn't enough; the *quality* of that time matters, too. As you begin to think in terms of bonding without breaking the bank, you'll start to see opportunities everywhere for creative, productive ways to spend time together. And you'll get better at making the moments count.

With awareness and minimal effort, you can transform the simplest errand or activity into a memorable moment. We love the idea of creating a special greeting, hand squeeze, or hand-clap routine that is unique to you and your child. Three squeezes in a crowded escalator means "I love you." A wink and a nod across the bleachers tell your budding athlete you're proud he hit the ball off the tee. It's something special, just for you. Decorate an ordinary moment with a tiny act of love and caring.

Bonding on the Go

With parenting, it's often the little things that are the most memorable. Here are a few ways to spend more time and fewer dollars. Invent some of your own.

- THE SHARING WALK. Not just any walk, the sharing walk is a special opportunity to talk about something special—sometimes celebratory, sometimes scary. Whether it's you or your child who initiates it, you both know it's time for undivided attention. No cell phones, no pets. Just the two of you talking about what matters.

- AISLES OF SMILES—THE GROCERY STORE GAME. We all have to go to the supermarket, race through the aisles, and rush home to drop off the food before heading to whatever is next. Slow things down, devote a little more time to the shopping trip, and see what a difference it makes. The grocery store game is not so much a game, but a fun way to enjoy shopping. Travel the aisles together, do the math to find the best deals, and fantasize about "what if" we could create an all-dessert meal or invite the president over for dinner. Focus on a particular ingredient, like additives. As you walk and shop, help your child learn to read labels to understand what's really in that peanut butter cookie or frozen macaroni and cheese. One day, you might challenge yourselves to choosing foods with no more than three ingredients on the labels. Explain to the kids that the perimeter of the store—protein, produce, and dairy— is where you should spend most of your time and money.

- **THE HAPPY BOX.** Find a nice box or decorate a drab one and name it "the happy box." When something especially delights you or your child, write it down on a slip of paper (or have your child dictate if he is too young to write). It's a way to count your blessings, a simple acknowledgement and celebration of what makes life good. On challenging days when perspective is lacking and someone is whining every five minutes, open up the box and read what's there. Help your child see patterns, for example, that the things that make Mom happy are often related to the happiness of the other people in the house. Over time, you may want to pull out the old entries and put them into an album. Seeing the changes over the years is really amazing, and you also make room for new ones.

- **SHOE-TO-DO BOX.** Another fun box project is to fill a shoebox with little treats and toys like a yo-yo, a deck of cards, a mini trivia game, a map of the world, a sack of foreign coins, a handful of Legos, etc. When the kids are looking for something fun to do, open up the box where a mini-treat awaits. You can use the box in lots of cool ways. Grab five items and use them to create a little play. Put them on a tray and make a memory game. It's simple, nearly free, fun, and delivers that little surprise element kids adore. Switch out the contents when the kids aren't looking. A great source for box contents is that shelf in the laundry room where you put random stuff rescued from pockets!

- **GROW-A-GARDEN.** This is simple and satisfying. Prepare a shallow plastic container, fill an egg container with dirt or till a little patch of earth. Plant a few perennial herb plants, a seasonal vegetable, or a pretty flower. Kids really get into watching over growing things. When possible, share your harvest with others. Attach a homemade sticker to a bag that says, *Jake's Home Grown.*
- **QUOTE NIGHT.** Designate a certain night as "quote night." Everyone comes to the dinner table with a favorite quote from someone they admire, a book, an online source, or something they overheard. These are recited and discussed in turn. This is especially good for older children, but you'd be surprised at how young the little ones can and will get involved. Of course, you can do the same thing with poetry or song lyrics. No doubt you've read interviews with highly successful people who are asked what made their home life special. None may have ever been involved in "quote night," but it's the kind of thing that makes a difference.

Turn On Your Fundar

Being ready for unexpected fun, or "fundar" as we like to call it, is one of the most intuitive things you can do in your quest for no-cost entertainment. It's a word you won't find in the dictionary, but should. And whether you set out (as many working parents do) a specific time of day for playing with your kids, or whether you've got the whole day together, you have to be ready for fun, positive interactions whenever they present themselves.

Fundar is a mindset. When your child wants to play hopscotch, shoot some hoops, or cozy up with a book, try your best to set other things aside. Of course, we can't (and shouldn't) say yes to everything our kids ask, but when they ask for time, try to say yes. You can never rewind that moment. As somebody smart put it, "Kids spell love T-I-M-E."

Don't miss out on those moments when your child wants to do something meaningful, purposeful, or even a little crazy. Many years ago, Evie was at a farmer's market with her friend, Marcia, and their kids. There was a stand selling old-fashioned candy sticks for a quarter apiece. Evie always remembers how Marcia (not an overly indulgent parent, just wise) put it when the kids clamored for a peppermint stick: "It's just so much fun to say yes." The same goes for those requests to do a craft, set up the sprinkler, or play the umpteenth game of Candy Land that week. You don't want to miss a moment of togetherness, a moment that could teach, inspire, or motivate.

A few strategies make it easier to maintain your Fundar:

Cargo ready

Keeping a few basics in the trunk of your car is a formula for spontaneous fun. First thing you'll want in there is an old blanket or quilt. The same one will serve perfectly well to cover the ground when you're at a T-ball or a soccer game at a bleacherless field. A blanket is also the first step in an instant impromptu story time outside the public library or a sun-drenched nap together in a local park. You'll also want to keep some basic sports gear in the car, depending on what sports your family likes. We always kept a softball and a couple of old gloves handy. A game of catch was a delightful way to pass time pleasurably with child A while child B was at a birthday party or lesson. Add in a small, boxed trivia game, a couple of chapter books, and a package of granola bars. In the summer, don't leave home without bathing suits and towels.

Mad money

Okay, we know this book is about not spending money, but you'll see from time to time that we simply have to dip into the piggy bank, and this is one of those times. Keep a coin purse in the car, in the bag you carry for errands, or even in the house. Throw a couple of dollars in from time to time—maybe change from a five-dollar bill, money you find under the sofa cushions, or quarters to recognize a child's kindness to someone else.

For absolutely no reason (or for a good reason if you prefer) decide that it's time to spend the mad money. Even if the amount is quite modest, it can be such fun to figure out what to do with it. A drive-through milkshake on a hot summer afternoon? A few lottery tickets if your family permits such things? An inexpensive bouquet of flowers to cheer up an ailing neighbor? Deciding what to spend it on can be as much fun as the spending itself.

Confessions of a Frugal Mom

Bobbi Burger Brunoehler of Los Angeles homeschools her kids for a simple reason—she wants more quality time with them. And even though Bobbi has plenty of marketable skills, her decision to stay home has meant less money coming in and more reason to live frugally. Here are a few of her suggestions:

- **Use the library.** Save thousands of dollars on books over your children's lifetime by relying on your local library. Bobbi goes to the retail bookstores, makes notes of what she wants, then checks her library's online catalogue. If what she wants isn't available, she orders it from another library.

- **Do the research.** Take the time to really look for free and low-cost stuff. When Bobbi's son was nearing driving age, she heard about a free defensive driving course run by nationally known race car drivers. The course was worth hundreds of dollars (there are a number of these on the market) and even included taking the wheel of a race car. It was not highly publicized and there weren't many available slots, but Bobbi nailed one for her son, who thought the experience was the absolute coolest.
- **Get to know your kitchen.** At the end of the day, it is cheaper and more healthful to cook than not to. Bobbi has started growing her own vegetables, and she's gotten really good at making ahead and freezing food, which gives her more time for her kids.
- **Start swapping.** There's much more on swapping in Chapter 5. Bobbi insists that it's ridiculously easy and satisfying to find great stuff without spending a penny, and it can be really fun to do with kids. She blogs about time, money, and other cool stuff at Bobbisbargains.blogspot.com.

Saving Your Sanity (and Money, Too!)

For anybody who's ever lost sleep over unpaid bills or high credit-card balances, it's easy to see the link between saving money and saving sanity. When we overspend and become obsessed with material things, we feel like our lives are spinning out of control. Sometimes, spending causes the feelings of craziness. Sometimes, feeling a bit crazed leads to too much spending. Either way, you can deal, and the trick is planning ahead. The goal, and it is possible, is to make saving money fun.

Okay, picture the late-afternoon scene at your house. Many families find the hours from five o'clock through dinner time quite challenging. There are just too many competing priorities, from homework to sports, clubs, errands, and more. If you're shepherding kids to lessons and activities, the most tempting thing to do is to blow twenty dollars on a couple sacks of bad takeout food. But by planning—and doing—ahead, you can beat Mr. Time Crunch at his own evil game.

If you've put something in the slow cooker in the morning, you've got the peace of mind that comes from knowing you're all set in the dinner department. And if you slow cook on low, you can leave it during a full work day. Similarly, make a double portion of baked chicken and freeze the second half for the super busy nights. It's not rocket science, and thinking like this can help you stay cool and resist money-wasting temptations.

Planning ahead in terms of activities is another way to keep the "spendies" from coming to call. When everybody's bored and on the way to fussy, the temptation to haul the kids (and the neighbors' kids) to lunch, the movies, or a skating rink is strong. Plan ahead by checking your city's newspapers and online calendars weekly for free family activities. Wherever you live, you'll find loads of choices—free concerts at a local college, special seasonal activities, bike rodeos, hikes, free days at the local museum, story time at the library, and more.

When Evie's family lived in a small New England town, the community sponsored free evening entertainment all summer in a local park. They'd pack up the kids and a picnic and head out a couple of nights a week. Even if the film, play, or concert wasn't totally kid-friendly and they had to leave in the middle (is there anything worse than a wailing toddler in the middle of a scary Bette Davis movie?), they were still ahead.

Another simple sanity saver involves your little coupon box. You'll be a lot less likely to overspend when you use coupons and "two-fers" for family entertainment. Keep the organizer up to date and don't leave home without it. (We suggest you keep it with the reusable grocery bags in the back of the car.) You'll be amazed by how much anxiety you can take out of an afternoon with the kids if you've planned in advance where you'll go based on what you have coupons for. And the same goes for those community dollar-saver books. They may cost ten to twenty dollars, but offer literally thousands in potential savings. Make it a habit to check the book every time you take off for an outing.

When it comes to food, planning ahead helps you find more time in your day for the important stuff. One family we know prepares a few meals together on Sunday evenings. They enjoy one then, refrigerate another for later in the week, and store a couple in the freezer. Speaking of the freezer, it's easy to avoid the "what's for dinner" craziness when you've shopped wisely, bought on sale, and frozen in meal-size amounts.

At a couple of dollars apiece, bags of pizza dough (most grocery store bakeries make their own) are simply brilliant. Stretch, roll, add cheese and toppings, make a salad, and dinner is served. And when rotisserie chicken is on sale, buy several, wrap them well, and freeze them for easy weeknight meals. Add frozen vegetables and a baked potato or shred them into tortillas. Take out or eat out? Absolutely not necessary, even on the busiest days.

Eager to break the eating-out habit, the Sampson family put ten dollars into a jar every time they considered heading to a restaurant but didn't. At the end of a year, they had saved more than two hundred dollars, and the family voted on how to spend it. Ultimately, the winning idea was to use the money for tickets to a world-famous circus. The Sampsons spent time together making and enjoying dinner, while they saved money and avoided lots of stress.

Piggy-Bank Thinking

Changing your approach isn't a magical overnight transformation. It happens the same way you fill a piggy bank—incrementally, a few coins at a time. But, interestingly enough, the disciplined habit inspired by a good, old piggy bank is actually one of the best money lessons you can teach your kids.

Children learn what they live, and when it comes to saving and spending, parents are, hands-down, the largest influence in their lives. So, when they see you save—in a jar, at the bank, and by doing with less—it sends a powerful message. If you need help explaining savings and the economy in ways children will understand, there are wonderful free tools out there to help you.

Information from the investment company Charles Schwab notes that a discussion with kids about savings needs to start with the basics—you save so you can have money for the things you want and need, and in order to avoid debt. Schwab urges parents to teach kids by example through the habit of "paying yourself first" by saving at least 10 percent of everything you take in (gifts, babysitting, part-time job, etc.). Check out these doable steps for teaching good sense about dollars and cents.

- **SET GOALS.** Work with your child on short (weeks), medium (months), and long-term (more than a year) goals, and a plan to get there. For a nine-year-old, a short-term goal might be the purchase of a book or a video. A medium-term goal might be the purchase of a watch. And a long-term goal might be buying a CD player. After you've set goals, talk about wants vs. needs.
- **INCORPORATE AN ALLOWANCE.** Although not all parents agree, Schwab believes that having one's "own" money helps a child understand lessons like compromise and financial trade-offs. A portion of the money should be saved.
- **BE OKAY WITH NO.** Belinda Fuchs, CPA and President of OwnYourMoney.com, makes a really simple but important point: it's okay—and even encouraged—to say no when you're out shopping. If young kids learn that the toy they play with in the store probably isn't coming home with them, they will handle it much better—as will 'tweens and teens when outfits or electronics have to be left behind. It's all about helping them learn to respect money and your limits in providing it.
- **START SMALL.** Even very young children can understand the idea of interest, which is why a savings account is more interesting than a piggy bank. Some financial institutions offer special children's savings products. (Make sure there are no fees

attached.) Some parents match kids' savings, which can really help the pot grow.

- **REVIEW PROGRESS.** Review bank statements to see how close a child is to meeting her savings goals. Reinforce the long-term benefits of saving.

If your child isn't quite ready for a savings account, you can help him understand interest with nothing more than a couple of cups and a handful of change. Mark one container with "S" for savings and the other with "I" for interest. If a child puts a quarter into the savings jar, put a nickel in the interest jar. At 20 percent, it's a high rate of return, but that doesn't matter. The idea is to teach kids that money can "work" for them.

If you have older children, you can have fun and learn a lot by playing the money-free "stock market" game. Everybody gets $1,000 in play money. If you don't want to steal from a game, make it yourself. Everyone "invests" in stocks of his or her choice. It's fun to research different stocks. Let kids check out companies that make things they like to eat, wear, and do. Track the progress of your stocks for three months. Assess how much everyone made and lost and lessons learned.

Another cool way to teach children about money is through a couple of very good websites just for them. Start at Treas.gov/kids (the U.S. Treasury's children's site). From there, click on the site of the U.S. Bureau of Engraving and Printing where they can design their own dollar bill, go on a treasury trivia hunt and catch a counterfeiter. They'll also enjoy the children's site run by the U.S. Mint (USMint.gov/kids), where they can learn about the history of the Mint through fun games.

While you're online, visit the site of Moneyopolis.com, a game developed by the accounting and consulting firm Ernst & Young for kids in grades 6–8. The game teaches financial concepts and incorporates a virtual city in which kids manage money and work toward goals.

Spend time, not money, and use some of that time to teach financial lessons to last a lifetime.

Memory Makers

Finally, before leaving the subject of "time, not money," we urge you to invest some of your own precious time in capturing memorable moments in your children's lives. Turn everyday objects into priceless keepsakes you can save, give as gifts, or use to decorate.

A finger-paint masterpiece becomes a beautiful work of art when framed and hung in a special place. Be sure the child's name and age are at the bottom. You'll treasure your pint-sized Picasso's work of art! Costly picture framing can become absolutely free when you recycle an old frame and use materials around the house for matting.

When Ali was born, Robyn's mom presented her with a beautiful photo of Robyn wearing her first baby dress. Robyn reframed it in a shadow box, framed Ali's first baby dress, and hung them side-by-side in Ali's room. She also pieced together remnants of baby and child clothing she saved—favorite socks, bows, and clothing—all in shades of pink from Ali's wardrobe as a child. If an outfit was stained, she cut out the stain and used a piece in the montage, and then used the rest along with other large pieces to make a gorgeous quilt that sat on Ali's bed for many years. Now both are treasured keepsakes Ali hopes to pass on one day.

Ready, Set, Go!

As you read more of this book, we hope you will begin to feel and embrace the *Eat, Nap, Play* parenting style. We want to help you enjoy raising a more independent child who knows how to be resourceful because he's seen you do it. Purposeful parenting that's fun and satisfying for you and your child? We're all about it! In Chapter 2, we're kicking up family time.

Mommy, Daddy, and Me— Family Activities

HERE'S NOTHING LESS COSTLY OR more valuable than family fun. It can be as simple as cleaning out closets with the kids and delivering outgrown toys to families in need. It might be movie night on the couch, or a late-night talk fest under the covers. However it's spent, time is the raw material from which memories are made and values shared. This adage says it all: *Spend twice the time and half the money on your children, and you'll be doing well.* We totally agree.

Parents are the most creative people on earth. This chapter is meant to inspire you to dig a little deeper. Rely on your knowledge of your children and their interests, and combine them with no- and low-cost resources like parks, playgrounds, and community activities. The little joys add up to big fun and fabulous family memories.

Teach your child the thrill of picking an I-planted-it-myself tomato or delivering a bouquet of wildflowers to a home-bound senior. Tour a local farm and see how cows are milked. Visit the local fire station where the children will have a blast climbing onto Engine Number 1 and learning important lessons about fire safety.

We've got both time-tested and all-new Mommy, Daddy, and Me ideas. Check out some smart tips for 'tweens and teens as well. Each precious moment spent with your child is a building block for a solid, connected future.

Early Imprints

As parents, we naturally expose our kids to our own interests. An essential part of their growing up (and eventually apart from us) is assessing those exposures and determining which interest them and which do not. It's no wonder great athletes and musicians often raise children who share the same passions. Certainly there is some "nature" in the passing of genes that produce great basketball players or tenors. But we believe there's a great deal of "nurture" involved, as well. Awareness and exposure often lead to interest.

That's not to say we believe everyone should encourage children to become mini-me's. Rather, we serve them best when we introduce them not only to the worlds we inhabit, but to other ways of living and creating. Spending time around parents and their pursuits can have interesting results.

For example, as an author, Robyn exposed both of her kids to book writing at early ages. It was easy to publish Justin and Ali's first books at a quick-copy store, binding the pages they had written and then illustrated with crayons and markers. She'll never forget the pride both felt in creating their own books, reading them aloud, and sharing them with Grandma and Grandpa.

As a result, both of her kids felt destined to write books. When Ali was faced with writing dozens of thank-you notes when she turned thirteen, she couldn't find a book that gave her good ideas. Robyn had written *The Thank You Book*, but it was for adults. So Ali decided to write *The Thank You Book for Kids* (www.thankyou kids.com) and (www.activeparenting.com). It was featured on national television, CNN, and in many magazines. Ten years later, it still helps kids find meaningful ways to express appreciation.

Similarly, Justin Spizman, who is now a lawyer, wrote a book about surviving and thriving in law school called, *The Insider's Guide to Your First Year of Law School: A Student-to-Student Handbook from a Law School Survivor* (Adams Media) www.beaninsider.com. Both Ali and Justin have also authored second books that benefit charitable causes. They grew up in a family that celebrated the art of writing, from simple thank-you notes and holiday poems, to letters from camp and college.

The takeaway is this—let your children see and feel your passions. They know you like nobody else. They're intimate with your strengths, and they certainly know your weaknesses. Put them in situations in which they can see you doing your thing. Let them get to know the "you" the world admires. Whether they choose to emulate you or are inspired to make very different choices, that is what this whole growing-up process is all about.

Trash to Treasures

You don't have to be a crafty genius to transform everyday junk or near-junk into timeless treasures. Teachers, challenged by tight budgets, are incredibly expert at turning a sow's ear into a silk purse, using daily discards to create fun and useful stuff. Start an odds-and-ends box where you can stash promising recyclables. Clean and dry everything first, and make sure there are no sharp edges or anything that could be hazardous to a child. Avoid small objects that might be choking hazards if toddlers will be involved. Some of our favorite junk:

- Bottle caps
- Yogurt containers and lids
- Packaging inserts
- Cardboard, and cardboard boxes and containers
- Buttons
- Pipe cleaners
- Twists and ties
- Labels
- All kinds of packing materials
- Stamps
- Stickers
- Egg cartons
- Washable fast-food containers
- Small assorted boxes
- Ribbons and bows
- Wrapping paper
- Hang tags
- Used, washed panty hose
- Greeting cards
- Paper towel rolls
- Colorful shopping bags

Saving odds and ends is also a strategy to teach recycling and repurposing. Kids love to see how simple, everyday objects can take on a new life. When she worked as an art teacher, Robyn would recycle the used paper from billboards (back when billboards were made from printed paper, not digitally scanned). "The way the words were composed of thousands of tiny dots reminded me of pointillism. These used-up ads helped me teach art history, inspiring my elementary school children to make gorgeous collages and designs from the dot-filled, colorful paper. I loved giving these discards a new life and saving money on expensive paper."

Check out some of these trash-to-treasure projects.

Paper plate pizzas

They look yummy, but these pizzas are not for eating. They are, however, much fun to make and a cute way to introduce simple fractions. Cut a crust out of brown or tan construction paper, glue it to the paper plate, then let the kids go crazy making cheese, sauce and all their favorite toppings—olives, onions, cheese, and pepperoni. When the creations are complete, everyone can cut their pies in halves, then fourths, and eighths as you introduce a simple lesson about fractions. Parts of the whole are so much easier to understand when you can see and touch them.

Another take on this is to use tissue paper to create a three-dimensional look. Tear the tissue into small pieces and scrunch it up into little balls. Or place a piece of tissue onto the eraser end of a pencil and twist it. The ends will stand up, and the flat tissue will become 3-D. Make an edge around the plate to serve as the crust, and then fill in with the other colors to look like tomato sauce and cheese.

This is fun to do on a night when you're planning pizza for dinner. When the kids are done playing with their paper pies, they can put them on the dinner table right along with the real thing.

Paper plate people

You'll need paper plates, non-toxic markers, construction paper, and your odds-and-ends box. Use one paper plate for the head and one for the body. To create arms and legs, use 12- to 24-inch strips of paper about 2–3 inches wide. Accordion-folded, the strips make jaunty arms and legs that can be glued or taped to the "body." Self portraits are always popular, as well as moms and dads with zany features and creatures from outer space.

Egg carton creations

Repurpose egg cartons into silly people. Begin with a clean, dry carton. Divide the carton horizontally or vertically (this works with cartons that hold a dozen or a half-dozen eggs) depending on the shape you'd like to end up with—skinny or squatty. You can also cut out individual sections to create ladybugs or other mini-insects. Use a glue that sets quickly to apply odds and ends like buttons, wiggly eyes, construction paper, etc.

Paddle ball

A DIY paddle game? You bet. Carefully shape each of two wire coat hangers into paddle shapes and tape over any sharp edges. Pull clean but slightly run (not shredded) panty hose over each frame and tie it off to create tension on the surface. Roll another pair of panty hose on the other frame, and you've got a pair of paddles and a ball. It's a fun indoor "sport," perfect for the basement or a big rec room.

Reporting for Duty

Sure, we're big believers in spending focused time with your child that's free from distractions. But at a certain point, work must be done, and kids love the feeling of being involved. Parents who work at home can set up a small desk or table that lets their son or daughter work alongside them. It's not highly interactive, but it's companionable and fun.

Supply your little one's desk with all kinds of stuff—pens, paper, paper clips, a stamp pad with a couple of stamps, scissors, old magazines, sheets of recycled cardboard, last year's desk calendar, a few used file folders, and pads or notebooks. If you've got an unused phone, keyboard, or monitor around the house, these digital castoffs are always a big hit in the "office." Make sure to provide plenty of recycled paper, crayons, markers, and pencils for art projects. Also good are check registers and checks from a closed account, as well as rulers, index cards, and highlighters.

From an early age, kids can be made to understand that sometimes Mom or Dad can talk during "work," but sometimes not. Evie was an at-home writer and single mom for years when her children were small. They learned that if they saw her phone headset on her head it meant, "Quiet, please. I'm on the phone." Or if she'd tap three times gently on the desk, it meant, "Quiet, please. I'm thinking, and I'll be with you in a minute." It worked . . . most of the time.

Make sure to build in coffee breaks or lunch time to your work schedule. Kids love this. Get yourself a cup of coffee or tea and mix up a mug of hot chocolate for your "assistant." Use the break to actually talk to your child about your work. Explain what you do in terms your child can understand and admire. (How often has the subject of "What does your mom/dad do?" come up, and a child will say, "I don't know." There's no reason for that. There's a kid-size explanation for almost everything.)

Fix and Make Stuff

Bob the Builder grew into a multi-million-dollar enterprise for a good reason: Kids of all ages love tinkering with and fixing things. You can have wonderful you-and-me time *and* knock off some projects around the house. If you've got an old, worn tool belt around, adapt it to fit your child. And, depending on his or her age, provide plastic or mini "real" tools. Do-it-yourself projects are fun and creative; they also teach resourcefulness and money-saving habits.

You don't want a four-year-old wielding a hammer and nails, but small children make great helpers. As you prepare for a repair, ask your "assistant" to help with tasks like these:

- Handing you tools and other equipment provided there's no safety hazard.
- Tearing out pictures from magazines that give an idea of how a finished project (painted cabinets, a new raised garden bed, or extra laundry-room shelving) will look.
- Doing light sanding.
- Painting up some old terracotta pots to give them new life.
- Picking up spilled screws and other clean-up tasks.
- Picking out matching pieces of wood for a woodworking project.
- Literally holding onto the top of your hand as you hammer (with the other hand well out of the way).
- Decorating rocks to place in garden beds.
- Shining or polishing surfaces with a rag and non-toxic product.
- Chronicling the stages of a project by taking digital photos.
- Gathering cut branches into a brush pile.

You also might want to consider working together on a special project for the child herself. Paint up a desk and chair you find at a yard sale and let your daughter decorate it with stickers, graffiti or painted designs. Or use stuff you've got around the house to create craft supplies. Who needs a store when you can create your own clay or Silly Putty? Try and share these recipes.

HOMESTYLE PUTTY

2 parts Elmer's Glue-All
1 part liquid starch

Gradually pour the starch into the glue and combine. If the mixture seems too sticky, add a little more starch. Cover and refrigerate overnight. The next day, your little DIYer will have a fresh batch of putty!

MODELING CLAY

Combine 2½ cups flour, 1 cup of salt, a cup of water and food coloring as you choose
Store in refrigerator and enjoy!

Love Your Library

If it's been awhile since you visited your public library, be prepared. The library you once knew has undergone an extreme makeover. You won't find the white sign-out cards and the stubby little pencils. But you will find computer access and a huge variety of fun, free offerings for all ages. For the voracious readers in your family, the good news is that the shelves are still stocked with books galore. And they're all yours for a swipe of your electronic library card and a promise to return them in a couple of weeks.

Lending libraries, which have been around since ancient times, are bursting with 21st-century technology and opportunity. From small town, one-room libraries to the multi-site libraries in our largest cities, you'll find fabulous resources and programs for children. Bring the toddlers for story time—some libraries offer an early-evening session where everyone comes in PJs—and take home a stack of board books. There are themed events and holiday parties, summer reading programs, movies, family nights, theater workshops, and music programs.

For older kids, the public library offers a safe, wi-fi environment, homework help, talking books, teen book clubs, cookie decorating, chess tournaments, and traveling exhibits. Some offer lending toys for visually impaired children. (And don't dare leave the library without visiting the adult department! Treat yourself to the many resources. At a sampling of libraries across the country, we discovered everything from writing workshops to knitting circles, online databases, scrapbooking clinics, downloadable books, and music and books on CD.)

Here are a few ideas to turn a trip to the library into a special occasion.

- **PACK A LUNCH.** If you're planning to attend a program, pick books, or use the computer, pack a lunch, spread out a blanket on the library grounds, and make it a special event.
- **TURN THE TABLES.** Get a stack of books and sit in a quiet corner of the library while your child reads to you. She'll love having your complete attention, without at-home distractions like the phone, the laundry, etc.

- **SUBJECT DU JOUR.** Before your visit, pick a subject on which you and your child would like to become "expert." Then use computers, magazines, and the ever-knowledgeable reference librarian to learn all you can about Jacques Cousteau, life in Uganda, how people live at the South Pole, or the history of ballet.
- **SHARE COOL STUFF.** If you've got a collection or something special you'd like to share with others, ask the children's librarian if you could sponsor an exhibit. It's fun for kids to see their own collection set up for everybody to enjoy. Preparation is fun, too. Get the kids involved in making little cards that tell about the items and the collectors. Evie and Erica did this with a small collection of antique dolls at a local library. They loved working on the display, and the patrons really enjoyed the exhibit.

Do Good Together

Open your heart instead of your wallet. Volunteering is a wonderful Mommy/Daddy and Me activity that can engage kids of almost any age. When Evie's kids were of pre-school age, she used to take them along when she delivered Meals on Wheels. The seniors were happy to have a warm meal delivered, but they were thrilled at the chance to visit with the little ones. It was a lot of in and out of the carseats, but the smiles on the seniors' faces when the kids toddled in made it absolutely worthwhile.

When the kids were slightly older, Evie changed her volunteer project to helping at a soup kitchen, where the children could be helpful arranging chairs, setting tables, and greeting the guests.

Children as young as three can understand what it means to help someone in need and to show respect in delivering the help. You could partner with your child to collect gently used sports equipment from the neighbors that could be donated to a youth center, collect clean, worn clothing for a shelter, or lead a can drive to help stock your local food pantry.

Many families engage in an annual service project, often around the holidays. Deliver a basket of food and hygiene supplies to a family identified by your house of worship or a local shelter. Lead a toy drive at your children's school. Show your kids what a difference you can make, together, by identifying a worthy cause and putting forth the effort. They'll get a sense of accomplishment and, hopefully, model the giving spirit as they grow.

Amy's Party

When she was thirteen years old, Amy Zeide of Atlanta wanted to donate a portion of the money she received at her Bat Mitzvah to help children in need. Working with her parents, she launched a holiday party for a handful of needy children.

The party has grown into a major annual event for hundreds of guests, including children and parents living in shelters, as well as hundreds of teen volunteers from throughout the community. Guests enjoy a carnival with prizes, arts and crafts, a professional DJ and dance floor, a picture with Santa, pizza and cake, and the opportunity to choose two new toys to take home.

Today, Amy is a wife, mom, and teacher. She is a firm believer in the power of kids and parents working together to help others. Although the party is an official project of Atlanta's Marcus Jewish Community Center, Amy and her parents still shop together for more than 1,000 toys each year.

Amy explains, "I think the holiday party became what it is today because my mom helped me foster a passion that she recognized in me before I fully recognized it in myself. She knew me well enough to recognize my interest in children, my passion for helping people less fortunate, and my skills in leadership and organization. She helped guide me toward something I would not only feel good doing, but that I would be good at doing."

There are endless opportunities to reach out. A good resource is the nonprofit group Volunteer Family. At its website, VolunteerFamily.org, you'll find basic information about family volunteering and good ideas about whom and how to help. VolunteerMatch.org is another well-known resource that pairs helpers with organizations in need. For parents who are already volunteering, it's often possible to find age-appropriate ways to involve your children in the work you're doing. As they get older and develop their own interests, as Amy did, support them as best you can.

As you consider a service project ask yourself these questions:

- What populations would we most like to serve?
- How much time can we commit each week or month?
- What do I want to get out of it, and what do I hope my child gains from the experience?

Dress-Up for Two

Dressing up is a magic carpet ride to anywhere for an imaginative child. And it's a fun way to spend time together. Does your home have a cozy little nook or other tiny space that could become a dress-up corner? Consider the space behind a stairwell or a safe, accessible crawl space. Hang an old sheer panel or some long beads and, if possible, install a low rod and hooks for hanging the dress-up clothes. You'll also need to hang an unbreakable mirror so everybody can properly primp.

Dig in your closet or attic for fun stuff. Old prom dresses, used-to-fit tuxedos, and uniforms are always prized dress-ups. Ask grandparents and other family members to see what they can find. You can also pick up a big bagful of wonderful things from garage sales, Goodwill, or local thrift stores. Look for the stuff on clearance tables.

Choose shiny, funky, off-size clothes, and don't forget hats, boots, and other accessories. Of course, if you have adult-sized clothes, avoid trip hazards by hemming pants, skirts, and dresses.

Boxed costumes (though we know you money-free fans can do better than those) go for next to nothing the week after Halloween. Check your big-box or discount stores to see if there are any great finds. If the clothing items cannot be washed, you can clean them with Dryel, the pennies-per-load dry-cleaning product that works in your clothes dryer.

Here are a few ideas to make dress-up an interactive activity to enjoy as a family.

- Help your little one dress up as a character from a favorite story. Sit together and read the story in costume.
- Encourage the kids to write a play that they can act out with

siblings or friends. Make sure there's a role for the dog and plenty of wardrobe changes.

- For a special treat, do the kids' makeup after they've dressed up as pirates, princesses, or wherever they've chosen. Make sure to take and share pictures.

Outside Interests

The great outdoors is the biggest, "free-est" source of fun on the planet. It provides endless opportunities for healthy ways for parents and kids to interact. Some families take bike rides in the country together. Others love to hike, fish, or roller skate. Some children and parents are crazily competitive when they play driveway basketball, while others never keep score. There's just nothing that feels quite as good as running around together outside.

Of course, what you do is all about your interests and preferences. But here are a few low-budget, high-reward things we've done and loved.

Set your sights high

Decide with your children on an outdoor activity goal you'd like to accomplish in the not-too-distant future. The older the child, the farther out you can plan. An example is your community's 5-K walk or run. If the event will take place in June, start training together in April by increasing the length of weekend walks until you're sure everyone can safely do a 5-K, which is about three miles. Decorate T-shirts to distinguish your "team" and make sure to bring fans to cheer you on. The combination of physical accomplishment and disciplined goal-setting is powerful.

Learn a new sport

Pick a sport that neither you nor your child has played much, like tennis, rock-climbing, or chess outside in the park. (Is that a sport? Well, you get the idea.) Take a book out of the library or study some YouTube videos to give you the basics of the sport. If equipment (like tennis racquets) is required, borrow it, and then if things go well, look for used equipment online or at yard sales. Set weekly dates to practice and enjoy your new-found sport.

Rediscover your first wheels

Most families have a few bicycles of various sizes in the shed or garage. But when's the last time you packed a lunch, strapped on a helmet, and covered some serious ground on your two-wheeler? Depending on where you live, you might have to drive the bikes away from city traffic. But it's well worth the effort to take a beautiful ride in the countryside or on safe sidewalks. Children as young as five or six, even with training wheels, can ride quite far, especially if it's flat. There's a huge thrill in coming home and announcing, "We rode ten miles today!"

Consider camping

You may not be the ultimate outdoors mom, but you don't have to be to organize a fun camping trip with your child. It's an especially great way for a single or non-custodial parent to spend one-on-one time in an intimate environment.

You might want to start with backyard camping. It's exactly what you think—pitch a tent in the yard and spend the night outside. Make this extra fun by "pledging" not to go into the house unless it's an emergency. The goal is to be organized about what you need, pack as you would for a trip farther from home, and stick to the plan.

You'll need a water-resistant, easy-to-assemble tent. You may have one gathering dust in the garage, or borrow from a neighbor before you invest. Alternatively, you can even stretch sleeping bags out on the lawn. (We highly recommend an air mattress or at least a tarp underneath.) There is a real thrill in staring up at the stars from your perch on the ground.

If you can't build a campfire due to local regulations, you can come close by setting up a circle of rocks and placing several lit flashlights in the center. It's the perfect setting for spooky stories, songs, and, of course, s'mores.

If "real" overnight camping is more your style, you're in luck. Even the most highly congested urban areas in this country are not far from state parks and private campgrounds. Once you decide on your destination, let your child get in on the choice of food, hikes, and activities. Depending on the destination, you may wish to hike into your campsite, hike to a waterfall or summit once you get there, canoe, kayak, or fish. Whatever you choose, camping is a top togetherness activity. It's a way to learn new skills and teach important lessons like how to read a compass and follow trail markers.

Keep in mind a few camping basics:

- KNOW YOUR SURROUNDINGS. Learn all you can about your destination before you get there, including expected weather, terrain, availability of services, and whether you'll have to "pack out" your trash.
- TAKE WHAT MATTERS. Be sure to pack needed medications for you and your child, as well as sunscreen, bug repellant, plenty of bottled water, and a basic first-aid kid. Leave the electronics

(other than a cell phone for safety), makeup, and favorite clothing items at home.

- **BE PREPARED.** Evenings that seem warm can turn into cool
nights. Be prepared with layered clothing, an extra set of socks
and shoelaces, books of matches in a waterproof bag, a pair of
whistles to signal your location in case you get separated, and a
plan about what to do if you find yourselves separated on the
trail. Be sure to tell someone exactly where you're going and
when you expect to return.

- **EATS AND DRINKS.** Safely storing your food can help you keep
a safe distance from wildlife, including bears. The National
Park Service suggests you hang food above the ground in bags
made for this purpose. Be careful about sampling berries,
mushrooms, etc., along the trail unless you are very familiar
with them. And avoid drinking from lakes and streams unless
you've brought along purifying tablets.

- **KEEP IT SIMPLE.** Cooking over an open fire is awfully fun, so even
if you bring sandwiches, fruit, and chips, you should plan to
build a fire for roasting marshmallows. Other easy meals include
hot dogs, hamburgers or veggie burgers, a pot of chili you make
at home and heat up on the campfire, or simple "foil suppers."
These are wrap-at-home foil packages of sliced chicken, veggies,
and potato slices that you cook at your campsite.

Just Me and My Teen

We love seeing a sixteen-year-old out with his mother. We think
there's something sweet about a tall teen towering over little mom
as they pore over the jeans and tees on sale at the mall or take in a
movie. The neat part is that they're together. As kids get older, it can

be harder to find easy ways to spend time. They get pickier about what they like to do . . . and with whom they want to do it.

Even if you have to plan fairly far in advance to accommodate work, school, sports, and other have-to's, put a "play date" with your teen on the book every few months. (Just promise not to call it that!) One fun way to spend time is to take turns indulging in one another's interests. If your daughter wants to do free makeovers at the department store, go for it. Next time, she can accompany you to a free showing of a classic movie.

Here are some other ideas for affordable hangin':

- **REDESIGN YOUR TEEN'S ROOM.** Let him take the lead, but be there for advice, support, and furniture moving as needed. Do it on the cheap by finding new uses for old items, painting over tired pieces, covering windows in creative ways, and searching yard sales for funky wall art.

- **COOK A MEAL.** Teens like to eat, and when they take the time, they like to cook, too. Invite the neighbors or the grandparents. Check out recipes on the Internet and enjoy kitchen time together.

- **PLAN A PARTY.** If you're cool with it, help your teenage daughter plan a party. Keep the costs down with a potluck menu and odds-and-ends decorating. Work together to plan and prepare the food, clean the basement, and design invitations. And, of course, be on hand, but maybe not so visible during the party.

- **SWEAT IT OUT.** Get on your bikes, walk around a nearby lake, or start running together. You'll be amazed at the quality of the conversation once the initial panting is over!

- **LISTEN.** Your teen wants you to know about his struggles and successes, even if he doesn't always let you know he wants you to know. Listen actively by sitting down together at a coffee shop (no cell phones allowed). Ask open-ended questions, verbally reflect what's being said, and ask questions to make sure you heard correctly. Don't try to "solve" every problem; sometimes they just want to know you're there. If the conversation gets a little intense, stay cool, be respectful, and expect the same behavior in return.

More Mommy/Daddy and Me Activities

We couldn't close out this chapter without adding a few more favorite Mommy/Daddy and Me activities:

- **BAKE A CAKE.** If you're a talented baker, share your skill with your children. But if you're not, at least make sure they know how to bake a cake from a mix. Robyn's daughter, Ali, learned this at a very young age and became known for her inventive cakes. When a friend had a down day, a pet died, or a neighbor had a birthday, Ali was right there with a special cake.

- **WATCH THE SUNRISE.** Wake your child early, have a picnic breakfast ready, and enjoy the sunrise together.

- **MOVE TO THE MUSIC.** Can you dance? If so, teach kids some "real" steps and let them teach you a thing or two as well. Kids are naturally great dancers, and it's such fun to move to music together.

- **CREATE A MINI-ENTERPRISE.** A family in Maine had a lot of fun and made some serious cash by investing in a used hot dog wagon that they took to fairs and festivals on the weekends. There were jobs for family members of all ages.

- **SET UP A PUZZLE TABLE.** Whether you have the space to establish a permanent puzzle table or you trot out a card table once in a while, puzzling is a great activity because you can talk while you search for pieces. It's a great antidote to television watching on wintry weekends.

- **YOU'RE INVITED!** As children get older their world expands to include special people who teach them, coach them, or mentor them in other ways. These relationships can often be quite formative for your child. If you're like many parents you remember these important adults at holidays and at the end of the year.

  But why not consider inviting a Scout leader or teacher to dinner or Sunday brunch? It's a memorable family activity that shows your child that people who are important to him are important to you. One family we know gave each child a chance to invite someone to dinner every year. The guests included everyone from favorite teachers to the owner of the local bike shop! These dinners helped forge new bonds with people who mattered to their children and were treasured by everyone involved.

  Let your child participate as much as he would like, starting with a hand-drawn or computer-designed invitation. Talk about the menu together. From discussions in class or on the field, your child may have some insights into what this special person likes to eat. And even though it can be quicker to do it yourself, make sure to involve your child in cooking. Nothing feels more gratifying than presenting a beautiful lasagna or chocolate cake and being able to say, "I made this for you."

  You can also think about an activity or entertainment to

complete the evening. If your child is the outgoing type, he might want to put on a puppet play, perform a song, or take the guest on a walk to a favorite neighborhood place.

The people who teach and inspire our children are often not the most highly paid people in society, though perhaps they should be. The imprint they make can last a lifetime. Recognizing their contributions is a feel-good activity long remembered by hosts and guests alike.

Another name for "mommy" might be "boredom-buster"! Don't despair. We've got ideas and inspiration in Chapter 3.

3

Mommy,
I'm (Still) Bored!

MOMMY, I'M BORED! Since time began (actually, probably long before), kids have looked to their parents to relieve the dreaded boredom. Play is a child's work, but sometimes it's hard to figure out how to have fun. The need to be entertained seems to last forever, but around age eleven, that starts to change (we promise!), with 'tweens spending more time independently.

That might sound like a fantasy now, though, as your world revolves around block-building and finger-painting. We've got ideas to make each day brand-new with creative car time, better baths, and more.

A New Way of Thinking

Avoiding boredom is a challenge for every parent, and it's even harder when cost is an issue. But, as you correctly guessed, it can be done. It's all about shedding that price-tag mentality and thinking on a whole different level. Here are some jumpstarts to get you thinking in a new way.

- **GO TO THE MALL.** The mall can be a great way to kill time, especially on a freezing cold or super-hot day. But too often an innocent outing results in a bunch of unanticipated charges on your credit card. So, what can you do to kick up a mall outing without the high cost? That could mean teaching pre-schoolers the correct way to stay safely nearby and not wander. Celebrate the great job they do with a stop for ice cream. As you walk, create a game of I Spy (a woman in polka dots, a man wearing a green shirt, a boy carrying a red shopping bag). Beat boredom by transforming your outing into a treasure hunt. Start early to discourage shopping and spending as default activities!
- **START A PLAYGROUP.** When Robyn's daughter was a toddler, she started a playgroup that met at a senior citizens' residence. A local newspaper thought it was quite inspiring and featured it, which attracted more young moms to join. The seniors looked forward to watching the kids play, and the children loved the attention from all the "grandparents" who welcomed them with open arms.
- **LEARN A NEW SKILL.** Learning to play the violin, ice skate, or speak a foreign language offers children tremendous benefits, but lessons can get expensive! Instead of the fifty-dollars-per-hour lessons and tutors, look for a high-school or college-age

neighbor to teach the kids tennis or hip-hop dancing. Not only will the kids be stimulated, they may find something they feel passionate about and want to master. Reciprocate with a few homemade meals, and everybody wins.

Read on for other boredom-busting ideas, including some guaranteed to help stave off the car crazies that can transform a leisurely drive into a full-blown meltdown.

More Than a Game

Kids are naturally talented at finding ways to stay occupied. With hopelessly little to entertain her, a child can turn a wooden spoon into a magic wand, or a deck of cards into 52 tiny train cars. But when boredom hits, it really hits, and suddenly their reserve tank of ideas is empty. From there, things can go downhill pretty quickly.

Beating boredom is not just about handing them complete ideas with rules to follow and expected outcomes. It's about teaching them how to stir things around differently in their own heads, looking at an old situation in a new way to come up with something fresh and, even better, free! After all, Frank Lloyd Wright's mom claimed that giving her son building toys helped him become one of the world's most famous architects. And the sculptor Alexander Calder created his own toys, contributing to the playful, inventive works of art for which he is renowned.

One of the best things you can do is to pattern productive ways to spend time. Do your kids see you sit down and read something other than a work-related report or a school lunch menu? When you've got a little bit of time on your hands, do you reach out to others, phoning an elderly relative or mixing up a casserole for friends who just adopted a baby?

Do you express yourself creatively through painting, cooking, singing, or woodworking? Remember how much art you used to do as a kid? Maybe it was simply coloring or making stuff out of clay. But artistic self-expression was just part of child life. Unfortunately, unless adults are especially "talented" or "professional artists," most of us lose our connection to art as we grow older. For no good reason, we stop doing what used to give us so much pleasure.

For yourself and for your child, don't lose your inner artist. If you reach for a set of colored pencils and some recycled computer paper, or sit down at the piano for fifteen minutes while lasagna is baking, your kids will likely do something similar. They won't end up doing just what you do, but they'll get the pattern. It's a special thing to be able to pick up a pencil and draw. Learning or perfecting a skill or talent feels good, and it certainly doesn't cost much or anything at all. Self-reliant, money-smart kids find ways to entertain themselves without spending. Same goes for their parents.

The notion that time is a gift is a pretty grown-up idea, especially to a child for whom a single summer day can feel endless. "After lunch" is light years away, and "tomorrow" is a whole night's dreams from now. But if we can get our kids to understand at age-appropriate levels that time is precious, it becomes easier for them to understand that it should not be wasted.

Like money, food, and other things of value, time is to be used wisely. That doesn't mean we turn our children into hyperkinetic machines who don't know how to kick back. Learning to relax and appreciate rest is another way of honoring time. Seeing time as a gift means living life to the fullest—discovering the joy of the moment and our capacity to be creative and productive.

And like so much about our less-money-more-time approach, keeping boredom at bay is a mindset. It's about the conscious decision to raise resourceful kids who will become resourceful adults, never afraid to try a new bike path, a new friendship, or a new recipe. A magazine on its way to the recycling bin becomes an art project. A to-be-discarded sock becomes a puppet. Look out, here comes fun!

Are We There Yet?

Whether you drive short distances, spend hours a day driving car pool, or accompany your kids on public transportation, your days can be filled with an awful lot of getting from here to there. Yes, riding in the car (and driving it!) can be *bor-ing!* But not if you transform drive time into an opportunity for learning and fun.

Quality family time does not have to take a back seat just because you're moving from place to place. Take the opportunity to find out—without all the distractions of home—about your children's day in school, state of mind, social challenges, etc. Use those hours to reinforce spelling, math, and other learning. Safety is what matters most in the car. So never initiate a game or activity that will distract you from driving! After all, in no time that little passenger secure in her booster seat will have her driver's permit. Sure, she'll take driver's ed, but the lessons she learns from you about sharing the road and staying cool are the ones she'll follow.

We post car rules on an index card in full view. Let your passengers know you mean business by communicating the importance of these rules. And that goes for friends and car pool kids, too.

- Buckle up as soon as you're seated.
- Keep your hands to yourself.

- Do not ever distract the driver.
- Use a quiet voice.
- Say thank you for the ride. (Personal pet peeve of ours.)

Games on the Go

Games occupy kids like nothing else. They also help kids and frazzled moms clear their brains. Games reinforce respectful behavior, waiting patiently for your turn, and not criticizing somebody else's answer. When the kids have exhausted their favorite games and look to you for new ideas, be ready.

- **GROW-A-STORY.** This game is a classic, but you may know it by a different name. Someone starts a story, and each passenger adds a sentence in turn, growing the story. Each player retells the story up until his or her addition, which adds a memory component. See if you can keep it going until you reach your destination. Older children love the additional challenge of moving through the alphabet for each addition. For example: "**All** of us went for a ride one day when the sun was shining and there were no rain clouds in the sky. **Brittney** said she wanted to go, but when we got to her house, she wasn't there!" And on it goes to Z, or until you get to the soccer field!
- **NAME GAME.** There are tons of ways to play around with licenses plates. One is the Name Game, sometimes called the License Plate Game. Challenge the kids to spell out their whole name—first, middle, and last—from license plates they can see. It's not as easy as it sounds, which is great because it can take miles to spell out the names of everybody in the car. The first person to spell his or her name wins, and everybody else has to

finish until the final name is spelled out. As is always the case with these car games, there's plenty of un-requested "helping" from other family members and, of course, the occasional, "You *did not* see a Z for Zoe!" Response? "Did so, did so." Okay, everybody, quiet back there!

- **I Spy.** This game is a great car, bus, or train tradition. There are lots of ways to play. In one version of the game, each child identifies objects whose names begin with the letters of his name spelled out. Justin spies roadside **junk**, then an **umbrella**, a **shopping mall**, and so on. The one who completes her name first wins. Then she gets to help the others spell their name until everybody has got it. In a twist on this, each child picks a color and has to find an object that spells out chartreuse or turquoise, which certainly keep things going longer than spelling out red and blue. Try to get color names with approximately the same number of letters to avoid the obvious claims of "unfair, unfair!" Suck it up and quit the whining, guys. Life's not always fair.

- **Name That Car.** This game is always a hit. When the little ones get antsy, one of the best things you can do is stop alongside a nice empty field and let them run around for ten minutes. But depending on where you're driving, it can be pretty hard to find a field. So the next best thing is a game that lets them release energy by getting silly.

  Each player makes up a name for a passing car, but the name has to include the color, like Cloud Blue or Ruby Red. It's great for those who are just learning their colors and are sitting up high enough in their car or booster seat to see out. You can also get a rhyme thing going, like Mellow Yellow or Brighty Whitey. For older kids, especially those interested in cars, challenge them to name the make of the car. Try this same thing working through the alphabet—**A** for Audi, **B** for Buick, **C** for Camry, etc. That ought to take you all the way across the country!

Love Those Big Brown Signs

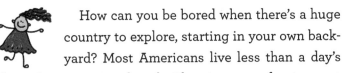 How can you be bored when there's a huge country to explore, starting in your own back-yard? Most Americans live less than a day's drive from a national park. There's a ton of enjoyment behind those big brown National Park Service signs. Start close to home for an affordable way to discover some of the most beautiful scenery in the world, plus presidential boyhood homes, historic sights, battlefields, trails, and so much more. Some locations charge a nominal fee; others never do. Start at nps.gov/parks and also check out the Park Service's excellent children's site, nps.gov/kidszone. Boring? No way!

Over the River *and* Through the Woods— Longer Rides

When the trip is longer than about four hours, you have to crank up the creativity to fight off boredom. Think about it—you're asking kids to stay cooped up for more than half a school day. Keeping everybody relatively quiet, entertained, and well-behaved becomes more challenging as the hours go by.

We've got a fun activity that recognizes the best-behaved child (or parent for that matter) as the Star-of-the-Car. An onboard snack is a good prize. Or prepare in advance a little homemade award that says Star-of-the-Car and the date.

Each child's name is on a list that's maintained by a non-driving adult. An episode of awesome behavior (cooperation, keeping hands to oneself, or speaking kindly instead of screaming when a backseat mate gets too close) is noted. The winner gets the award, such as his or her first pick of snacks.

Long trips can feel endless, and they really are hard on little kids with short attention spans and abundant energy. Helping them understand how far you're going and how long it will take can help. Do it by giving them a visual image of the trip in the form of a familiar animal. Let's say you're embarking on an eight-hour trip. Before you leave home, go online, print out a big image of a giraffe, for example, from Google Images and paste it on a piece of cardboard.

Indicate the beginning of the trip at the tip of the giraffe's head and the destination at the bottom of the giraffe's leg. Then mark the time as you move slowly down the giraffe's neck, back, hind side, etc. Choose a horse or a dog for a shorter drive. Let the kids indicate on the animal where they were on its body when they stopped for an ice cream or ate a picnic lunch. Bring time and distance into a kid's sphere of understanding, and you just may develop a more patient traveler.

Here are some fun and fabulous games for car fun:

- **WHAT WOULD YOU DO?** Open-ended conversation games encourage children to think strategically. Someone starts by asking, "What would you do if you were stranded on an island with food, water, but no electricity, no books, and no boat?"

Or, "What would you do if you could time travel back to any moment in history?" Or, "What would you do if you were principal of your school for a day?" It's an engaging way to stretch the imagination. And because the subjects aren't real, your child may be more open about sharing than if you asked a direct question about his or her life.

- **TALKING HIGHWAY.** This game sparks the brain cells. Imagine all the things you see along the road that can't talk, like trees, signs, buildings, lights, cars, the windshield, dirt . . . you get the idea. Each player chooses one of those silent objects and becomes its voice. In turn, the billboard, abandoned car, blossoming cherry tree, and spotted cow tell their own stories. You can count on an hour or so of good, brain-engaging fun.

- **WHAT'S THE WORD?** Ask your child to think of a word but not say it out loud. Then you supply a goofy word that the child will substitute for the word that's in his head. Say his word is "play," and the replacement word is "Popsicle." The winner is the first one to guess the real word that's being replaced by the word "Popsicle" based on what the player says. So, the child offers sentences like these: "I like to *Popsicle* (play) on the playground. And I really love to *Popsicle* (play) with the dog after school! And even though Mom may not like it, the best is to *Popsicle* (play) in the backyard when it's dark outside." The first one to guess the secret word gets to start the next round.

- **MATH ON THE MOVE.** Numbers are everywhere you turn during a long ride. Put them to good use with a fun little game you can adapt to any age and build your child's age-appropriate math skills. If you see the number 55, as in miles per hour, on a road sign, ask a pre-schooler to add the two numbers. An answer of 10 equals a point. For an older player, ask for the answer of 55 x 4 within a given number of seconds. Closest or right answer wins. And, yes, parents are allowed to have pencil and paper, but not the kids!

- **COUNTDOWN.** Pick a number, say 50 or higher. Those playing have to count up (or down) from that number by spotting the numbers, in order, outside the car on billboards, road signs, license plates, and so on. The first person finds the number 1. The next person has to find a 2, and so on. The goal is to see how far you can get while traveling. One family we know exceeded 100 many years ago, and despite lots more traveling and playing, their family record still stands. If anybody can remember where you left off, you can pick up the game on the next trip.

- **HAPPY TOGETHER.** This is a simple, sweet game that can be played by anyone who's old enough to talk. You go around the car and fill in the blank: "I am happy when . . ." The first player says: "I am happy when I eat ice cream," and the next one says, "I am happy when I eat ice cream and there are two scoops." The next says, "I am happy when I eat ice cream, there are two scoops, and my brother gets some, too." The game continues until someone messes up on the recitation. That person is out, and then everybody else continues to compete.

Trip Tips

 Here are some great trip tips supplied by our friend Dawn Dawson-House, Director of Public Relations and Information for the South Carolina Department of Parks, Recreation and Tourism. People like Dawn know a lot about car travel!

- **Chill.** In the car or at the destination, you've got to realize that vacation is by definition less structured than regular life. Don't flip out if things get a little crazy (outside or inside the car), and your kids will be much calmer in return. Pull off to the side of the rode if safely possible or don't start the car until the kids are calm. Safety first.
- **Make movies special.** Dawson-House thinks you should make DVD movies a treat. Instead of hitting "play" the minute you get in the car, build anticipation and make it fun by first setting a "show time," getting settled with snacks, then starting the movie. Simply put, drag it out.
- **Move by moonlight.** If the adults in the family can make it work, travel with babies and really young children at night. Make sure everyone has his or her own blanket to accommodate temperature preferences (and to reduce the number of potential squabbles).

Waiting in Line

Lines can be awful for kids. They're boring by design, and standing in them can be hot, cold, and/or exhausting. Lines seem to bring out the whiny worst in kids *and* parents. So, how do you teach a child to entertain himself rather than getting into trouble while waiting for a movie, parade, or special event? A game is a good way to keep the focus away from the event or activity you're waiting for.

You can adapt lots of car games to the standing position, like naming things that start with each letter of the alphabet. Lines also present great opportunities for an impromptu spelling or geography bee. If you don't have enough players, engage some near you in line—with parents' permission, of course.

Because you don't have your hands on the wheel, you can do a lot more to keep things lively. If you think you might encounter a line, throw some little items in your bag, such as small pads of paper, a handheld game with the sound off, binoculars, and a snack. A pack of pipe cleaners provides a mess-free craft. Also old-school but fun are string games like Jacob's Ladder or Cat's Cradle. Pack a little ball of string and craft scissors, or cut lengths at home and toss them into a plastic snack bag. One mom calls Silly Putty the great line whisperer when her kids go a little nuts.

Our kids always loved contests, like who-can-stand-on-one-foot-the-longest and, of course, the classic blink game (first to blink loses). Lines are a good excuse to get physical. In-place follow the leader is fun. And the classic head-shoulders-knees-and-toes can be remixed with different body parts for a nice stretch.

Bath Time

Kids naturally love water play, and baths are a perfect excuse for wet fun. There really should be a law against boring baths. With little effort, and certainly no money, you can make sure that your child's bath is fun, relaxing and, of course, gets the job done. Safety trumps fun at all times. Absolutely never take your eyes off a child in the tub. A few other bath time basics:

- A child under about age six should never (as in *never*) be left alone in the tub or under the supervision of another young child.
- Prevent potential burns by setting your household hot water heater at 120 degrees Fahrenheit. Fill the tub before the child gets in and make sure the little ones understand they may *not* touch the faucet handles.
- If you use baby seats, rings, mats, and other bath aids, understand that these are for convenience, not safety.

Need money-free ideas that can make a boring bath bubble over with fun? You've come to the right place:

- **FLOATER OR SINKER?** Gather a collection of recycled plastic containers that only come out at bath time. Nearly anything washable, plastic, and not too tiny can be interesting. Keep them in an open mesh bag (often used as a laundry bag) hanging over the tub to be sure they dry thoroughly between uses. And periodically run them through the dishwasher or hand wash to get off the soap scum. Kids have a natural engineering talent—they love to measure, fill, pour, and repeat. It's also fun to float a Styrofoam tray in the tub and see how many things can be stacked before the whole thing comes tumbling down. If you're bathing two kids at once, let the competition begin!

- **USS SOAPY.** Plastic or Styrofoam egg cartons make great bathtub boats. Rinse an egg carton well, then cut off the top to create a neat little boat. Depending on how actively the kids play, the boats may have a fairly short life before they're headed into the recycle bin, but not to worry, they're easy to replace.

- **TUB CASTLES.** Similarly, clean half-gallon or gallon plastic milk jugs transform nicely into floating castles. Cut them down (make sure there are no uneven edges) so the kids can stock them with plastic figures, animals, etc., to create their own little water town. The castles will actually float on a Styrofoam tray. (If it's been used for food, be sure you've sanitized it by running it through the dishwasher.)

- **SPONGE FISH.** We love taking a few clean sponges and cutting them out in the shape of fish. They make scrubbing much more fun.

- **MATH IN THE BATH.** A nice soak is a great time for some simple math games. Start with counting for toddlers, and advance to times tables and story problems for the older kids. It's also fun to "write" a number on a little back with soap and have the child guess it.

- **LITTLE SQUIRT.** Clean squirt bottles are tub-wonderful. Squirting is one of those activities kids like and parents usually frown on. But why? Kids love to feel they're doing something just this side of naughty. And there's no better place to squirt one another or towers of toys than the tub. Collect squirt bottles of different shapes and sizes and bring them out occasionally for a special treat. The same goes for bubbles. We've got recipes for making your own in Chapter 6.

- **EVERYBODY IN.** Once in a while, let the kids take a bath with some of their own washable dolls and toys and "bathe" them.

Don't expect the kids to get too clean; this bath is mostly for fun. And don't put any really filthy toys in there; save these for a big bucket outside on a hot day. But young children will enjoy washing and lovingly drying their "babies," and you'll enjoy knowing your kids are playing with cleaner toys.

Bedtime

Boredom is often a result of repetition and routine, but when it comes to bedtime the predictable can make for a peaceful and welcome time of day. So be careful not to overdo the boisterous fun and games while you keep bedtime fresh and interesting. Here are a few ideas that can easily be adapted to your family's routine.

- **MELLOW OUT WITH MUSIC.** Use bedtime to introduce your child to classical music, but keep the tunes restful—Brahms rather than Wagner, for example. Spend ten minutes together listening to a DVD. Cuddle up as long as they'll let you or just sit together without talking on the bed or the floor and soak in the music.
- **DO THE SAME WITH POETRY.** You can even designate one night a week for this, with each of you coming prepared with a poem or two to share.
- **LEARN A HANDCRAFT TOGETHER.** Those same ten or fifteen minutes before bed can be a fun time to do a handcraft with your child, such as knitting or crocheting. No stress, no need for perfection, just a restful few minutes.
- **ENCOURAGE JOURNALING.** For some people, including some very young ones, keeping a regular journal is a means not only for self-expression, but for self-understanding. Many new jour-

nalers prefer pen and paper to a computer screen. If your child likes the idea and wants to try it, assure her that what she writes is private. Too young to write? A picture journal is the answer.

• **STUDY OR PRAYER.** The last few minutes before hitting the pillow are a wonderful opportunity for learning or reflection. If you read from the Bible or another religious book, a brief study period before bed can set the right tone. Or you might like to choose a topic to learn about together. One family got totally interested in Harry Houdini. They borrowed several library books and spent a few minutes each night learning about this legendary magician. The solar system . . . Africa . . . ice-climbing . . . American Indians . . . you can never be bored if you're learning.

Timeless Treasures

As our children grow, their memories are best sparked by something we can see and touch—the clothespin mail holder, the ceramic elephant paperweight, and, of course, photographs.

Some of us are great at compiling these memories in albums and frames; other people (okay, Robyn) are great at turning bits and pieces of childhood into treasured keepsakes. For some moms, saving memories in scrapbooks is a joy, but for others it's a huge hassle. The key is to find your signature style and embrace it. Don't feel badly that your photographs are in a shoebox. Let the kids help you sort through them.

Scrapbooking can be a double boredom buster. It's engaging while you're doing it, and the result provides memories for a lifetime.

Scrapbook and craft stores are full of wonderful things (and a great source of ideas about page layout, etc.), but they can be expensive! If you're patient, you'll get the knack for saving bits and pieces of things that don't cost a dime. For example, before you send all those shiny, colorful mailers to the recycling bin, take a good look through them and hold onto those with images that could work for your page. Here are some other ideas for items that can be used for scrapbooking:

- **STAMPS.** Save cool-looking stamps from letters and invitations. Even the postmarks make a colorful way to date scrapbook pages.
- **RESTAURANT POSTCARDS.** Some restaurants have free postcard displays typically advertising products or even nonprofit services. These images may be just right for a scrapbook page.
- **INVITATIONS.** Save invitations to special events and birthday/holiday cards from parents, grandparents, and other special people.
- **PHOTOS.** Gather up some of those extra photos lying around (including duplicate school and sports photos) that aren't worthy of a picture album. Let your child cut them up and use them to illustrate a special event commemorated in the scrapbook. Add photo faces to stick figure bodies to bring the pages to life.
- **OLD BOOKS.** Instead of using a traditional scrapbook, scrapbook over another type of book of the size and shape you like, like an old coffee-table book that nobody looks at anymore. This is a fun transformation and a good way to repurpose old books.
- **MISCELLANEOUS.** Designate a shopping bag for each child and drop in relevant "stuff" that will make its way into the scrapbook. These can be things like ticket stubs and programs from a performance, a note from the Tooth Fairy, report cards, a school lunch menu on your child's birthday, and the invitation to Grandma's 80th birthday party.

Be sure to involve the children from an early age in creating their own scrapbook. Get their opinions about what events in their lives are most important to preserve. And let them go through the box and help organize stuff from a particular period or a particular part of their lives, like everything from first grade or from four years of ice-skating lessons and competitions. Then work together on laying out the pages.

Many people prefer online photo storage, but if you've got a mountain of prints, stop waiting for the perfect time to get them into an album. Years ago, we liberated ourselves from the idea that photos have to be perfectly, chronologically arranged in an album. Get to the dollar store, stock up on cheap albums, and get to work.

If you've lost track of when a photo was taken, label the book "Nick's Baby Years" and don't worry about it. You'll feel great getting the pictures behind plastic where they can be enjoyed. Talk about an antidote to boredom—kids are great at organizing if you give them a specific task. Working on photos is a way to spend quality time with your child. Conversation about the captured memories is always special.

We also love the idea of living with your photos by using them as décor. Save money on artwork and enjoy the fun of creating timeless treasures. Try these ideas:

- **CREATE A WALL OF FAME.** Designate a wall in your home where you display favorite photographs of family members. Plan the wall on paper so you know what you want to hang where. You can use matching frames or, more affordably, enjoy the eclectic look of unmatched frames. Use a mat and spacers to keep the glass off the photograph; this lets you more easily remove the photo from the frame when it's time to change things up.

Otherwise, the glass can damage the photograph. There are lots of YouTube videos that can teach you the basics of photo framing. Robyn always notes on the paper backing of each framed photograph the names of those pictured and the year the photo was taken. Keep your eye out for picture frames at yard sales and antique stores.

- **A DOZEN PRICELESS MEMORIES.** You'll never regret the time you invested in this craft. It's a way to chronicle your child's school years in a single framed photo collection. Select a favorite photograph of your child starting in first grade and insert it into a mat with twelve openings. Add one photo each year. Hang it on the wall and don't worry about the openings; it's a work in progress. One day, it will make a beautiful gift to give your child to show how he's grown throughout the years.

A Skill That Keeps on Giving

Kids who are parented creatively learn to entertain themselves in interesting, creative ways, and they grow into hobby-loving, passionate teens and adults. They know that the secret to enjoying the time we have on our hands is *in* our own hands.

We're playing with our food and loving it in Chapter 4. Keeping it healthy and affordable can be a blast, and we'll show you how.

4

Fabulous Food and Kitchen Fun!

EEDING THE FAMILY GOOD, NUTRITIOUS FOOD is one of a caring parent's biggest jobs. But most parents are starved for time! Let us show you how to do it more quickly, for a fraction of the cost, and more enjoyably. Bake without cooking, serve breakfast for dinner, and let the kids try their hand at meal planning. Lose the fast-food habit and get something much more memorable in return: kids who enjoy eating well for less at home sweet home!

Healthy Helpings

"Mommy, can I help?!" Kids are a natural in the kitchen. When you capture and encourage your children's involvement, they enjoy

the experience of eating together, shopping for food, and being your kitchen sidekick. Like the best chefs, kids are free-spirited, creative, and love mixing textures and colors. The best way to create healthy eaters is to make cooks out of them. With just a little thought and planning, you can help them discover a whole new world of fun and accomplishment.

We know the dinner hour can be one of the craziest times of the day, but making the effort to mix the kids in with the ingredients is a great togetherness technique. In our world, food becomes affordable fun. "Survive at five" is what most moms call it! Do more than survive—thrive during meal time.

The goal with kids and meals is to make food fun. It starts early with your baby and toddler and the mealtime patterns you establish. Is it all mess and stress? Is getting your child to eat an annoying challenge? If they see that you don't like to cook or are stressed at mealtime, kids will often reflect the same attitude. And if they feel forced to eat something, count on resistance. A positive environment and involvement in what you eat and cook will encourage a happier food experience.

Celebrate kids in the kitchen and feel better about the whole food thing with ideas like these:

- **KID PICKS.** When possible, let your child pick the veggies for dinner from the produce drawer or freezer. That means washing the produce, cooking, and seasoning it. Watch how many more green beans he eats when he "picked" them himself. Toddlers love to help snap beans. And they're awesome at tearing lettuce. Use Popsicle sticks to "cut" and "spread."
- **VEG OUT.** We're told that half our plate should be filled with fruits and veggies. So ask the kids to decorate dinner-size paper

plates to indicate what spaces should be occupied by salad, broccoli, fruit, etc., and which are for proteins and starches. Put them on the table and compare them to the way your real meal rolls out. The color, shape, and texture of veggies make them kid-friendly. Encourage your toddler to name the veggies as you wash and prepare them. Betty Broccoli is a silly but fun way to "relate."

- **TABLE FOR TWO?** Let the children take turns being the server of the night. That means bringing the food to the table for the rest of the family (supervised if needed), refilling glasses, and bringing condiments, a clean fork, or whatever else is needed. As at a restaurant, it's the server's job to understand and describe the food being served. (And, of course, offer freshly ground black pepper!)

- **FAKE FAST FOOD.** You absolutely can prepare a "fast-food meal" without the cost, fat, and preservatives. Sit with the kids at the computer and search the Internet for recipes for the fast-food items they love most. Be sure to add the word "healthy" to your search, such as "healthy chicken nuggets." Do the same for "fries," "shakes," etc. Tasty, homemade versions of all their favorites will pop up. Have the kids pick a name for their restaurant and decorate take-out bags.

- **OUR VERY OWN COOKBOOK.** Find a three-ring binder around the house and pick up some 8.5" x 11" plastic sleeves. Make category tabs for appetizers, main dishes, sides, and desserts. Each time you try a new recipe, write or print it out and add brief notes about who particularly liked the recipe, anything you did to change it, etc. Depending on their ages, the kids can help type and print, put the recipes in the right category, and decorate the pages. They'll love returning to a favorite recipe that *they* helped make. Name the recipes you try after the people who made and loved them.

You've heard it before—studies show that eating dinner together at home is one of the best ways for families to stay healthy and connected. Add your own table traditions to make dinner special. The same is true for preparing meals. You may not create any mini-Julias or Emerils in the process, but you'll have great, no-cost fun while the kids learn about healthful cooking and are more eager to taste.

Clip, Plan, Eat, Repeat

Teach kids about shopping and meal planning while reminding them that meals don't magically appear on the table! The food has to be selected, bought, and cooked into a healthy meal that everyone in the family will eat and enjoy.

It starts on Sunday morning after the newspaper has arrived. Gather all the coupons in the center of the table, plus any collected during the week from magazines, mailers, or the Internet. You'll need plenty to make this work.

Each reading-age child gets a batch of coupons and age-appropriate scissors. You'll also need a stack of inexpensive paper plates and several plastic kitchen bowls. The kids clip any coupons they like and place them in kitchen bowls labeled with sticky notes— main dishes, side dishes, breads, snacks, and "other stuff." The kids can mark the paper plates for "breakfast," "lunch," and "dinner." The number of each depends on which meals you expect to make or eat at home that week.

Taking turns, each child picks a coupon from the bowl and reads aloud what the item is and what meal it's for. If everyone agrees (you get the last word!), the coupon is placed on the appropriate paper plate. When all the coupons are placed on the plates, you've got the basis for the week's meals. Using the coupons, the children write the components of each meal on the paper plate and add up the coupon savings. You take the actual coupons, file them in your organizer, and shop for the agreed-on items.

The next part of the activity is to decide together what else you'll need to complete the meal (like salad, fresh veggies, bread, milk, and other non-coupon items). Write this on the paper plate, too. Then assign a day of the week to each breakfast, lunch, or dinner. For example, pot roast, oven potatoes, and frozen veggies might be good for a Sunday or holiday dinner because the roast takes several hours to cook. Microwave French toast is good for a school/work day breakfast, but homemade blueberry pancakes are a better choice for a Saturday when you have time.

Ask for a child to serve as "special helper" for each dinner and write that down on the paper plate, too. He or she helps set the table, cook, serve, and clean up. Older kids can contribute in a big way by making salads, assembling casseroles, etc. (Jobs help kids develop responsible attitudes toward being part of a family. Doing chores for your child accomplishes nothing. As they grow, their expectations about what you should be doing for them grow, too.)

In less than an hour, you'll have a week's worth of meals planned and a nice stack of money-savings coupons ready to use. Involving the kids in meal planning can also be an exercise in tolerance. Emma hates fruit salad, but Jeremy loves it. So you compromise by keeping both lasagna, which Emma loves and Jeremy hates, and fruit salad on the list.

Some families take the actual coupon savings from each shopping trip and put the money in a special jar. At the end of six months or a year, call a family meeting and decide how you'd like to spend those hard-earned savings—dinner in a restaurant, an afternoon of roller skating, or maybe some new DVDs!

Meals in Minutes

30-Minute Meals made Rachael Ray a household name, but lots of busy families don't have even a half-hour to devote to cooking. We get this. How is it that moms used to have all the time in the world to chop, shake, and bake? Today, there's so little time for galley duty, but delivering affordable, healthy meals is hugely important. If you find yourself struggling in this department, talk to other moms to get ideas, recipes, and inspiration.

Good cooks rely more on approach than on actual recipes. Make these totally easy ideas your own based on how and what your family eats, and how and what you want them to eat.

Breakfast

Who said breakfast has to be cooked in a frying pan or eaten at the kitchen table? There's a world of choices out there that can be made and eaten on the fly.

- **THINK OUTSIDE THE CEREAL BOX.** Robyn got three-year-old Justin to eat whole-wheat cheese toast by naming it "circus toast." She divided the toast into four sections, alternating different-colored cheese bits on each section. Toast became a colorful treat that Justin gobbled up.
- **BREAKFAST SANDWICHES.** Sure, you can go with fried egg on white toast, but why not change it up with peanut butter and honey on whole wheat, or almond butter and thinly sliced

apple on raisin bread? Any way you slice it, you've got low-cost, portable nutrition to start the day.

- **"INSTANT" CEREAL.** Make double the amount of rice (white or brown) for dinner and turn it into a delicious morning cereal. Heat rice for a couple of minutes in the microwave and top it with milk and a little brown sugar. It's filling and yummy!
- **ADD A SPECIAL PLACE MAT OR FLOWER TO THE TABLE TO BRIGHTEN THE DAY.** Robyn named it the thank you flower and let it act as a reminder for the kids to say thank you for the meal.

Lunch

Are you one of those people who have eaten a turkey sandwich every day for the past four years? It's easy to get into a lunchtime rut, and the same goes for your kids. Kick it up with a fun, different lunch that takes minutes to make.

- **PACK IT UP!** For a day-care or school lunch, pack cheese chunks and crackers separately. Fill a sandwich bag with *crudités* (French for cut-up vegetables), and toss in a mini container of dressing for dipping (like the ones you get from takeout meals). Add fruit and a couple of cookies.
- **ON A ROLL.** Experiment with roll-ups. They're versatile and pack really well. The bread comes in lots of flavors and sizes, and the fillings are limitless. Does thinly sliced leftover beef with shredded cabbage and spicy mustard sound good? How about sliced deli chicken, cheese, and dried cranberries?
- **ALL-WEATHER PICNIC.** Taste the fun of a picnic in any weather by spreading a sheet on the floor and picnicking indoors. Preschool kids love this. Let them help pack everything in a basket for the long trip from the kitchen counter to the floor.

- **BUILDING BITES.** Grab a stack of Legos. For every bite your child eats, a piece is added to the tower.

Dinner

We're living proof that you don't have to spend more than fifteen minutes preparing dinner when you pre-plan and shop ahead for meals like these.

- **SCOUT-INSPIRED SUPPER.** Spend a little and get a lot when you create a chicken-in-foil packet. Tear off a nice-sized piece of heavy-duty foil and coat it with cooking spray. Add a slightly pounded chicken breast, a couple of tablespoons of Greek (or other favorite) salad dressing, a thinly sliced white or sweet potato, and a handful of fresh green beans. Season with a little bit of olive oil, salt, pepper, and garlic powder to taste. Wrap well and grill for twenty minutes or so until the chicken is cooked and the veggies are tender.
- **PRONTO PARMESAN.** On spaghetti night, cook an extra box of pasta, drain it, and refrigerate it. A couple of nights later, you're minutes away from Pronto Parmesan. Layer spaghetti, jarred sauce, prepared chicken patties, mozzarella, and seasonings to create a delicious casserole. Top with Parmesan cheese, cover, and bake at 350 degrees for about twenty minutes or until bubbly. Delish.
- **GOOD MANNERS NIGHT.** By taking one dinnertime each week to teach, reinforce, and show off table manners, you can avoid constant comments and corrections. Instead of creating a negative climate for eating, this gives you one night a week to get your point across.

Cereal Box Champions

Back in the day, parents and teachers believed that self-esteem was one of the most important factors in a child's success. Now, some experts think we've gone overboard, heaping too much praise on our kids. They're critical of ideas like no grades on school assignments, and no winners or losers in sports contests. Some research shows that excessive praise may even prevent some kids from reaching their potential.

Wherever you are in this debate, we think our Cereal Box Champions idea is a very special and appropriate way to say "way to go." This quick craft makes your little one special without burdening him with too much of a good thing. Best of all, it costs absolutely nothing.

Here's how it works: When a box of your child's favorite cereal is empty, dust out the box, remove the wax bag, and cut out a portion of the front of the box. This cut-out section will be replaced with a photo of your child. Decide where and how much to cut based on the design of the box. Be careful not to discard any part of the box, as you'll want to put the two pieces back together as seamlessly as possible. Blow up a photo on the computer to size, colorize it online or by hand, glue it onto the cut-out portion, and put it back into the box. You may want to Photoshop the photo to include an object (like a soccer ball or violin) that reflects your child's special interest or success. Laminate it if you want, but it's not essential.

Now take a new box of the cereal, carefully lift the wax bag out, and slip it inside the redesigned box. You'll delight your child (and we hope not overly embarrass her) when you set this box of cereal out on the breakfast table.

In case your family doesn't eat Wheaties and your kids don't know about the Breakfast of Champions, explain the tradition to them. (The brand was introduced in 1924 by General Mills. Because it has always been associated with sports, Wheaties is known as the Breakfast of Champions. Over the years, Wheaties has recognized hundreds of winning athletes, sports, and Olympic teams by featuring them on their boxes.)

Compare the price of our no-cost Cereal Box Champions idea with the forty dollars or so you can spend to get an "official" likeness of your kid on a box of Wheaties. (Really, you can!) That's a lot of boxes of cereal and gallons of milk!

Faker Baker

If you're like us, you love the idea of serving fresh, wholesome baked goods, but who has the time to produce pies, cakes, and cookies from scratch? Becoming a Faker Baker is the answer. It's our way of saying, "Take it easy *and* take the credit!"

This is a great activity for a rainy or down day, whenever you and the kids need a little jolt of fun and a tasty treat. The idea is super-simple—no-bake, no-oven, easy-to-make sweets. That means even the youngest bakers in the house can participate. Plus, you won't heat up the kitchen or run up your electric bill. The other thing we love about these recipes is that you don't have to go out and buy all kinds of expensive ingredients. You'll find several that use things you've probably got in the pantry, and they're essentially goof-proof.

COOKIE CRUNCH BALLS

12 sandwich cookies

¼ cup milk

8 tablespoons peanut butter

1 tablespoon honey

Crush the cookies, add the rest, roll into balls, chill and enjoy!

ICE CREAM CONE SUNDAES

Ice cream

12 flat-bottom ice cream cones

1 cup chocolate or butterscotch chips

Sauces (Check your refrigerator door; you've probably got a few.)

Toppings (granola, nuts, sprinkles, etc.)

Melt chocolate chips gently in the microwave (about two minutes on 50 percent power), stirring after a minute. Brush some of the chocolate or caramel along the sides and bottom of each cone; refrigerate briefly to harden. (This helps it hold up to the ice cream and makes it taste good.) Now comes the cool part: Layer the ice cream, chips, and toppings in the cone, then top them with sauce and put them back in the freezer until they're solid. What a great way to use up bits of cookies, nuts, and bottom-of-the-bag cereal! They're even awesome for birthday parties.

YUMMY CHOW

(requires a microwave for melting, but no oven)

1 12-oz. box Crispix or similar cereal
1 cup peanut butter
½ cup butter
1 12-oz. bag chocolate chips
1 lb. box powdered sugar

Melt the butter, peanut butter, and chips in the microwave until smooth. In a separate large bowl, add the cereal, then pour peanut butter mixture on top; stir carefully to coat the cereal. Put powdered sugar into a large, zippered plastic bag. Add the coated cereal and close the bag tightly. Shake gently until the cereal is covered. This makes a delicious snack or dessert. Supervise the microwaving; hot butter can burn.

NO-COOK BANANA PUDDING

1 large package (6 oz.) vanilla pudding
2½ cups cold milk
1 14-oz. can sweetened, condensed milk
1 16-oz. container whipped topping
2 or 3 bananas, sliced
40 vanilla wafer cookies

Prepare pudding according to package. Stir in condensed milk and blend well. Fold in half the whipped topping. Make layers of pudding, bananas, and wafers, then top with remaining whipped topping and banana slices. Refrigerate several hours or overnight. Everyone will love this smooth, sweet treat with an old-school flavor.

Snack Attack

With their ramped-up metabolism, kids need constant refueling, but don't forget the adults in your house when it comes to good snacks. A quality nibble can help eliminate grazing if you're at home or hitting the dreaded vending machines at work.

Okay, snacks are great. But who decided that they should be expensive, wrapped in plastic, and marked with a shelf life well into the 2040s? There's a world of fresh, satisfying snacks out there that cost next to nothing to make at home. Try some of these alternatives. You can feel really good serving these to the kids.

- **YOGURT SUNDAE.** Scoop a cup or so of good quality plain or low-fat vanilla yogurt into each person's bowl. (Get the large container—it's cheaper and "greener" than buying individual plastic cups.) Arrange bowls of cut-up fruit, nuts, all-fruit spreads, and healthy cereals on the table and let the kids go for it, adding their own mix-ins. Who needs the processed yogurt parfaits when you can create a personalized, healthful treat at home?
- **PANINI PLEASERS.** Panini (grilled, Italian-style sandwiches) are hot, hot, hot. But you don't have to get on a plane or even buy a fancy panini maker to enjoy them. Grab a slice of any type of bread (even if it's not the freshest). Top it with your choice of meat, cheese, herbs, vegetables, and mustard if you like. Add the second slice of bread. Lightly spray a fry pan, turn to medium heat, and drop in the panini. Cover with a plate and weigh it all down with a teapot or whatever you've got handy. Cook 3–4 minutes on one side, flip, and then cook for another few minutes. (If you want to indulge in the professional panini

maker, consider what two sisters did to save money. They purchased two different gadgets—a panini maker and a waffle
maker—and shared the appliances.)

- **QUICK 'N CRUNCHY.** Lunch-takers love this. Mix together 3 cups
of mini pretzels, 4 cups of any Chex cereal, 4 cups of Cheerios,
a jar of roasted peanuts, ⅓ cup of melted butter or margarine,
a few tablespoons of grated Parmesan cheese, and salt and pepper to taste. Arrange everything on a cookie sheet and bake for
about 30 minutes. This yummy mix keeps great in an air-tight
jar. Happy trails!
- **"FANCY" CRACKERS.** Spread low-fat cream cheese or peanut
butter on each of six crackers. Top each with a single chocolate
chip. Our kids loved this treat when they were little—there's
just something fun about that little chocolate chip! Even toddlers can make it.
- **SOUPER EASY.** When it's chilly outside, there's nothing like a
mug of soup. Start with boxed or low-sodium canned broth
(beef, chicken, veggie, whatever you like). Then get creative by
adding handfuls of leftovers like diced meat or potatoes, last
night's green beans, cooked pasta, etc. Let the kids experiment
with seasonings like shake cheese, dried basil or curry. Cook
over a low heat until simmering. For just pennies you can stir
up a delicious, soul-warming cup of goodness.
- **FREEZER PLEASERS.** Got ripe melon around but nobody to eat
it? Don't let it go to waste. Freeze small, cut-up pieces of can-
taloupe, honeydew, or both. Remove the fruit from the freezer
and run it through a juicer to make a super-healthy, refreshing
frozen treat.

Make It and Take It

Life gets a lot more costly when family activities include eating out. There's money to be saved and fun to be had when you make and take food with you. And we're not just talking about a picnic in the park here, although there's nothing more fun or affordable than eating from a basket on a blanket.

We're talking about adding convenience and reducing cost by bringing instead of buying wherever you're heading—to the kids' sporting events, the movies, errands, or family visits. Drive away from the drive-through and try a smarter, better-for-you way to eat on the fly.

Whether you're heading to swim practice or the pediatrician, the key to making this work is getting organized. If your outing will occur around a mealtime, plan ahead, devoting fifteen minutes or so to assembling a meal from home and packing it up. Get the kids to help. Give the older ones some freedom, within boundaries, by leaving a basic list of what's needed (four sandwiches, a fruit or veggie side and something to drink).

You'll also want to be orderly about how you pack. It's well worth the investment to buy a decent cooler that keeps food fresh and prevents sandwiches from turning into pancakes. Keep a supply of paper plates, napkins, and cups in the car so you don't have to pack these essentials with every Make-and-Take meal. Save by using wrapped sets of unused plastic ware from previous take-out meals. You'll also want to keep a stash of trash bags (recycled grocery store plastic bags are perfect) in the car. All these staples can be stored neatly in a small box in the trunk for easy access.

One other must-have for off-road repasts is a quilt or blanket. We've set up many a lunch in a field, playground, or parking lot because we had a clean, old quilt with us at all times. The quilt doubles as a seat during softball and soccer matches. After use, give it a good shake or drop it in the wash, and then put it right back in the trunk for next time.

A picnic on a sunny spring or fall day is the best. But you really can do Make-and-Take meals in any weather or season. Carry your picnic into a mall, a community center, or skating rink. It's also fun and cozy to "dine" right in the car on a healthy homemade lunch before dropping off the kids for music lessons or between Little League and a Scout meeting.

And don't forget Make-and-Take for you and your honey. If you're headed for a PTA or homeowners' association meeting, turn the evening into something more by packing a lovely dinner and eating it first alongside a lake or other favorite spot. It may not be the most romantic idea in the world, but let's face it, date night can't always include a little black dress and a dimly lit restaurant.

Take home on the road, and save a fortune in fast food when you bring your own.

Mixing It Up

Hamburgers for breakfast and omelettes for dinner? Why not? Especially if it's nutritious, fun, and doesn't cost an extra dime. There's something about the idea of eating traditional foods at non-traditional times that kids really love. It helps spice up weekday meals and break up the routine.

Some families might consider steak and eggs for supper, but that's as far as it goes. We like to kick it up. Sure, it might take a few extra minutes to boil up a pot of pasta and slather it with your favorite sauce before the school bus comes. But what fun the kids

READER/CUSTOMER CARE SURVEY

HEFG

We care about your opinions! Please take a moment to fill out our online Reader Survey at **http://survey.hcibooks.com**.
As a **"THANK YOU"** you will receive a **VALUABLE INSTANT COUPON** towards future book purchases
as well as a **SPECIAL GIFT** available only online! Or, you may mail this card back to us.

(PLEASE PRINT IN ALL CAPS)

| First Name | | MI. | Last Name | |

| Address | | | | City |

| State | Zip | | Email | |

1. Gender
- ❑ Female   ❑ Male

2. Age
- ❑ 8 or younger
- ❑ 9-12   ❑ 13-16
- ❑ 17-20   ❑ 21-30
- ❑ 31+

3. Did you receive this book as a gift?
- ❑ Yes   ❑ No

4. Annual Household Income
- ❑ under $25,000
- ❑ $25,000 - $34,999
- ❑ $35,000 - $49,999
- ❑ $50,000 - $74,999
- ❑ over $75,000

5. What are the ages of the children living in your house?
- ❑ 0 - 14   ❑ 15+

6. Marital Status
- ❑ Single
- ❑ Married
- ❑ Divorced
- ❑ Widowed

7. How did you find out about the book?
(please choose one)
- ❑ Recommendation
- ❑ Store Display
- ❑ Online
- ❑ Catalog/Mailing
- ❑ Interview/Review

8. Where do you usually buy books?
(please choose one)
- ❑ Bookstore
- ❑ Online
- ❑ Book Club/Mail Order
- ❑ Price Club (Sam's Club, Costco's, etc.)
- ❑ Retail Store (Target, Wal-Mart, etc.)

9. What subject do you enjoy reading about the most?
(please choose one)
- ❑ Parenting/Family
- ❑ Relationships
- ❑ Recovery/Addictions
- ❑ Health/Nutrition
- ❑ Christianity
- ❑ Spirituality/Inspiration
- ❑ Business Self-help
- ❑ Women's Issues
- ❑ Sports

10. What attracts you most to a book?
(please choose one)
- ❑ Title
- ❑ Cover Design
- ❑ Author
- ❑ Content

TAPE IN MIDDLE; DO NOT STAPLE

BUSINESS REPLY MAIL

FIRST-CLASS MAIL PERMIT NO 45 DEERFIELD BEACH, FL

POSTAGE WILL BE PAID BY ADDRESSEE

Health Communications, Inc.
3201 SW 15th Street
Deerfield Beach FL 33442-9875

FOLD HERE

Comments

will have bragging that "My mom lets us have spaghetti for breakfast!" And, of course, you'll want to make sure everybody gets dessert before heading out.

If you're especially pressed for time, let the kids make a breakfasty dinner of cereal, milk, fruit, and toast. They'll love the silliness and the opportunity to "cook" for the family. You can also take toaster or microwave pancakes and pre-cut them into hearts. Why not keep the morning theme going and have everybody come to the dinner table (that means you, Mom and Dad) in pajamas? Everyone arrives dressed for bed, but it's mealtime instead. Perhaps dessert includes reading a few pages of *The Very Hungry Caterpillar*, a classic by Eric Carle, with the rest of the book completed at bedtime.

Use these idea starters to turn things around at your kitchen table:

- **FOR AN ENTIRE WEEK, FORGET EVERYTHING YOU KNOW ABOUT WHAT GOES WITH WHAT. COMBINE FOOD IN NEW AND FUN WAYS.** It's liberating and a great way to use leftovers. Okay, full disclosure—our spaghetti omelettes got mixed reviews, but the hot dog tacos (lettuce, salsa, and cheese toppings, of course) were a huge hit. Get the family involved in planning fresh, fun combos.

- **IF YOUR CHILD IS STUDYING A PARTICULAR COUNTRY IN SCHOOL, RESEARCH TYPICAL FOODS AND TRY MAKING THEM AT HOME.** Depending on the region, you could end up with some very unusual tastes. It's a great way for the kids to get the idea that different people do things in very different ways. The Japanese love soup for breakfast, and the French eat cheese for dessert. Why not?

- **HELP THE KIDS LEARN WHAT CONSTITUTES A HEALTHY MEAL BY CONSULTING THE UPDATED FOOD PYRAMID.** (MyPyramid.gov

makes the recommendations easy to understand, even for pre-
schoolers.) Plan a meal together that's nutritionally sound, but
one that mixes things up a bit. For example, try great grains like
quinoa instead of white rice and fun-to-eat veggies like eda-
mame (tender pods of baby soybeans that kids seem to love).

- **MIX IT UP IN LUNCH BAGS AND BOXES.** A baked potato topped
  with beans and cheese is a great alternative to a turkey sandwich, especially if your child or spouse has access to a microwave. Forget that boring packaged cookie. Try a yummy
  graham cracker and peanut butter sandwich. Or pack a frozen
  container of yogurt. It keeps everything else cold and makes a
  semi-frozen lunchtime dessert.

Proud-of-You Plate

Parents are always looking for ways to let kids know they've done
a great job without bribing them or appearing to "pay" for accomplishments. It's a fine line, and any parent lucky enough to have
seen a prized finger painting come home from preschool knows
what we're talking about.

An approach we love is the Proud-of-You Plate. You can take
this in all kinds of directions, but the basic idea is that your child
makes and decorates a special plate. This can be painted pottery,
hard plastic, or a real china plate decorated with permanent marker
and glued-on "gems" or cutouts, laminated photos of favorite
activities, etc.

Once the plate is completed, it's kept by Mom and Dad in an
undisclosed location and brought out to mark special occasions like
winning the spelling bee, making the soccer team, or super-cooper-
ative behavior. Like any treat, the key to making it meaningful is to

not overuse it. There's plenty of criticism out there of parents who over-praise their children for everything they do, which can make it hard for them to operate in the real world. Whatever your views on all that, we know that kids thrive on positivism in all of its forms. For some families, the emphasis is on academic achievement, while others like to reward kindness to others. The plate is a neat little way to say, "Hurray for you!"

Use the plate in fun and unexpected ways. You can certainly set it on the dinner table (use a cake plate stand if you've got one) to mark a game-winning point or a hard-won A. But you can also take it to Grandma's house where the family is gathering for dinner and surprise your child with it there, in full view of all the cousins. Or, if it's pizza night at a local pizza parlor, make sure the plate goes, too.

It's also fun to honor your child's accomplishment with a token. If Beth gets elected president of her high school's Habitat for Humanity club, slip the Proud of You plate on her bedside table after she falls asleep. Stick a note on it that exempts her from dish duty for the week to mark the occasion! Let Evan know you're proud that he can ride a two-wheeler without the training wheels by presenting him with the plate topped with a handful of his favorite candy.

The Proud-of-You plate lets kids of all ages know you're there to support them and encourage their efforts. Who knows, maybe they'll pass it on when they become parents!

A Note About Groceries

We agree with CPA and all-around money expert Belinda Fuchs that there are lots of ways to combat the high cost of groceries. Here are some of her tips for cutting the monthly food bill.

- **CHECK-OUT CHECKUP.** Sometimes even the smartest of us tend to underestimate how much we're spending at the grocery store. It's no wonder. You're trying to gather coupons in the line, and your ears are filled with, "Please, Mommy, PLEASE buy me the cereal with the gummy bears in the box, and I'll never ask again!" Not sure when we'll get back to the store and pressured by the kids, we tend to overbuy. The problem is, things that looked like a good idea get tossed. Fuchs suggests finding the time to get to the store more often, while staying efficient in your purchases.

- **BUY WHAT YOU'LL EAT.** The five pounds of peaches you bought on sale looked like a great money-saver. But eating two pounds and tossing the other three because they rotted before you could get to them isn't such a bargain after all. The same goes for buying at the warehouse clubs. They are fabulous and we love them, but it's easy to get eyes-bigger-than-head syndrome in those bigger-than-life aisles. Try the large-size containers a couple at a time. If nothing gets thrown out, buy it again. Consider sharing bulk purchases with another family. This way you get the savings without having too much of a good thing.

- **LOOK FOR VALUE.** Is a brand name product really better than a cheaper or generic one? Take a taste test and involve the family. And, for heaven's sake, read the labels. It's still shocking—and actually kind of annoying—to see large-size products priced higher per ounce than smaller packages. Hello?! We can do the math.

- **UNBUNDLE.** Ask your spouse or a neighbor to watch the kids while you go to the grocery store. You'll be more focused, tend to buy less, and deviate less from that shopping list. Certainly, let the kids get their votes in for what they'd like, but when it comes to the grocery cart, parents rule.

- **BUDGET.** There is no better tool than a shopping budget. If you're planning to spend $50, consider a 10- or 15-percent overrun, but more than that you simply hand back to the checker with a smile. Many people have gone to cash over credit cards as a way to control spending at the grocery store, and other retailers for that matter. If you're used to whipping out the plastic, it really feels different to know that you are absolutely limited by the amount of green in your wallet.

- **GAMES. THEY'RE MORE THAN FUN.** We love games for lots of reasons, including the fact that they're engaging, fun, and instructional. When you play games with your children you teach them many things, including all-important life lessons like waiting their turn, respecting others' time and space, and cooperating with teammates. Games teach math and reading skills, spatial awareness, decision-making, and strategic-thinking. As an antidote to boredom, there's nothing better than a rousing round of *Boggle*, *Memory*, or chess!

  Explore games as a way to teach and inspire kids in meaningful ways.

  Check out the Chicken Soup for the Soul game *Count Your Blessings* (countyourblessingsgame.com), a wonderful way to encourage your child to take stock of what really matters. Co-creators Laura Robinson and Elizabeth Bryan have created a meaningful and fun game that encourages kids to appreciate all that they have. Visit the game aisle to discover an affordable, cozy way to spend time together.

  Why not take gamesmanship to the next level and create

your own game?! You'll find great ideas online by searching "how to make your own board game." There are free board game-creation tools at the website of the Jefferson County, Tennessee school district, jc-schools.net/tutorials/gameboard. htm. You'll find goodies like a printable spinner, a board game template, and easy ways to create game cards. At the website helium.com click on the menu option "board games" for lots of good how-to articles.

Older kids may enjoy creating their own arcade or video games. Here, too, the Internet is a great resource. Take a look at stormthecastle.com or visit *YouTube*; there's lots to see and learn there.

- DECIDER-IN-CHIEF. If you've got a nice chunk of time on your hands, say three hours in the late afternoon, introduce the Decider-in-Chief activity. One family member gets to be the decider, choosing activities, food, or movies for everyone else to enjoy. It's a kicked-up version of follow-the-leader but much more fun and engaging. Kids love this because it gives them some of the power they associate with parents. It teaches them how hard it is to make family decisions that please everyone. And they see the benefits of a cooperative attitude when, the next time the game is played, another family member is in charge.

- THAT'S OUR SONG! Break out of the same-old, same-old mode by creating your own family theme song. Yes, this is crazy, but crazy fun. If you've got little ones at home, keep it simple by changing the lyrics to familiar songs, such as "Someone's in the Kitchen with *Sari* or *Brandon*." Post-kindergarten-age kids can easily rewrite an entire song. Search the Internet for the lyrics they want (they're all on there!) then encourage them to substitute new words that reflect your family's habits, quirks, etc.

If you or a child have a little bit of musical ability, try your hand at creating original music *and* lyrics. Most families have at least one member who can accompany everyone else on the piano or even a kazoo. Pop or rap music may come to mind first, but encourage your child to consider other types of music, including folk and opera!

Creating your own song is a neat way to bond as a family while encouraging kids to get involved in the wonderful world of music.

- PUT YOUR HEART INTO ART. An art-filled home is an exciting place to be, especially when the artists live there. Find new and fun ways to create and display family artwork. You may be one of those fabulous moms (we so admire this!) who are brave enough to whitewash a wall in your child's room and let the kids design and paint their own mural or graffiti wall. Another idea is to mount a large piece of corkboard in your entryway or mudroom and devote it to school and home art projects.

  Get out the non-toxic watercolors or acrylics on a nothing-to-do Sunday afternoon and paint portraits or try your hand at caricature or still life. Kids are much closer to their authentic inner artist than adults and doing artwork together is a great way to channel this natural ability.

So, now that you have our take on feeding your kids well while you have fun and spend less, we're heading to a very different place—the swap and barter world, where cash is definitely not queen.

5

Swap, Shop, Barter, Share

TALK ABOUT A FABULOUS WAY TO SAVE! There's an entire universe of swapping, bartering, buying secondhand, and sharing out there so vast it makes you wonder if anybody's buying full-price retail anymore. From a one-time family book swap to ongoing babysitting co-ops and kids' clothing exchanges, the opportunities are endless, and endlessly creative. There are all kinds of online bartering sites, school and neighborhood service exchanges, community cooperatives, and even one green plant swap we learned of.

The idea is as old as people and their stuff. It's all about the strong likelihood that something you want is the very same something that somebody else wants to get rid of. Your discard becomes somebody else's prized possession. Kids know it as, "I'll trade you half a peanut-butter-and-jelly for half a turkey-on-rye."

What's new is the upsurge in opportunities, largely fueled by the Internet. This chapter delivers the how-to on swapping, shopping, and other ways to find great stuff without overspending. Learn from some world-class swappers who love the goodies-for-no-money part, but are equally into the fun of it all.

It's a Movement!

CNN.com recently called swapping "the new shopping," and it's a pretty spot-on description. Some people have swapping in their blood; others discover the joys later in life. Artist and designer pablo solomon (he prefers no capital letters) grew up in poor neighborhoods in Houston. His parents put a high value on education, hard work, and discipline. "They also taught me the arts of bartering and of buying and selling," pablo told us.

"We bartered for anything and everything—stuff for stuff, stuff for work, and work for work. Some of my best memories are working with my dad to fix old furniture and with my mother to identify collectibles in order to sell or trade them. We always made extra money through bartering and selling." These frugal ways paid off. Eventually, solomon's parents owned their own home and had money in the bank.

Savvy Swappers and Shoppers

The variety and diversity of swappers is astounding. Rebecca is a writer, wife, and mother of six living near Houston. She and a group of friends from church use swapping to get more out of life than they might otherwise be able to afford. Once a month, a few moms go on a fun adventure and take another mom's kids. They babysit for each other during the day and occasionally during the evening to give another couple a date night ("anything from a romantic dinner to Christmas shopping for the kids").

The group also hands down kids' clothes. Several of the moms are accomplished seamstresses, so alterations are no big deal. The women even share special-occasion outfits. "And sometimes," says Rebecca, "we swap cleaning and laundry chores or loan our older children out as helpers for a day. It's funny how they love to clean at someone else's house, but not their own!" Because most of the families home-school, it's easy to share teaching materials and exchange kids for various lessons.

Kate is a California mother of two who is part of a group of three swapping girlfriends. Their Swap-Sit provides a few hours of babysitting on Monday mornings. One week, you've got seven pre-schoolers to watch over; the next two weeks, you've got a free Monday morning to shop, clean, work, etc. Kate does a similar swap for evenings out and has also started a food swap. Each member of a group of four makes a homemade food item to share. They've enjoyed everything from chocolate ice cream to lentil soup and quiche, all made from scratch, all made to share.

Twice a year, Kate hosts a Swap-Soirée. Friends pool their no-longer-wanted clothes and "shop" for gems from someone else's closet. "It's free, fun, and good for the earth, the closet, and the wallet," she adds.

In Colorado, home-based working mom Jessica swaps childcare duties with another mom so each gets in a full day of work. A serial swapper, she and her husband also created a ski co-op with friends. Participating families meet at a local ski lodge at a given time. Parents take turns skiing on their own while other parents watch over the children.

Cambridge, Massachusetts, mom Tara has scored loads of great stuff for her son over the years, from books to a tennis racquet, craft materials, and a prized night light for reading in bed. When she's done with something she's swapped for or finds she can't use it, she makes a point to donate it to her son's school. She's also gotten some great grown-up toys, like beautiful beads to make jewelry and a touring bike in mint condition for her boyfriend.

So Many Sites, So Little Time

Some people believe so strongly in swapping that they've created websites and online communities to share what they know about bringing people and their stuff together. There are enough sites on swapping, sharing, and buying used to fill an entire book, so we'll describe a representative few, the people behind them, and the special place they hold in the swapping universe.

Swap-bot.com

Rachel Johnson and her husband are the owners of Swap-bot.com, which they created in 2005. We love the way Swap-bot provides parents and kids with fabulous opportunities for creative self-expression. That's because the swaps on the site are all user-created, and they focus on all kinds of fun stuff, especially hobby and craft projects. One of the most popular categories is "mail art." Kids and their parents (you have to be 18 to have an account) create decorated postcards, sometimes around certain themes, and swap with other people doing the same.

Whether you're trading postcards, baby clothes, or other items, the website randomly assigns you a "swapping partner." You get their things, and they get yours. Rachel says lots of swappers end up connecting with their swapping partners, which is one of the most fun aspects. "The social component is really strong. We also have a forum and a chat room where people talk about crafts and life," she says.

If you can make it, you can probably find it on Swap-bot.com. Categories include everything from chocolate bars to fabric squares, homemade Barbie outfits, hand-decorated cardboard squares, and paint pails filled with various things. Users are encouraged to create their own swaps, and do they ever! At any given time, there are hundreds of them going on.

Swapitgreen.com

Margaret Mix is an experienced website builder who's turned her digital skills to the swapping world. Swapitgreen.com was created in 2009. It gives trading points for goods posted on the site. The points can be used to purchase other things. The site charges a nominal processing fee of 10 percent or less. People trade for everything you can imagine—books and DVDs, homemade jewelry, GPS systems, computers, sports gear, and more. If the item is available on Amazon.com, Swapitgreen will automatically download product information and a photo as a convenience. If not, the seller posts a photo.

People assign trading points to their own items, and playing fair is the name of the game, Margaret tells us. If the number of points assigned is too high, you probably won't get rid of your items. Collected points can be used when and how you want, a few at a time or all at once. "The whole idea is to recycle stuff rather than throw it in the trash, which is good for the environment, and get something in exchange that you can really use," says Margaret.

Swapgiant.com

This site was started by frequent Craigslister Joseph Denton. It's totally free and, in Joseph's words, "very grassroots." Swapping categories include babies'/kids' items, bikes, books/magazines, electronics, video games, sporting goods, pets, and vehicles. He's also got a section on wedding products and services, which are increasingly popular in the swap world.

Bobbisbargains.blogspot.com

Bobbi Burger Brunoehler is a veteran swapper and yard sale-er who has turned her experience into a popular blog. Bobbi has swapped, shared, and bartered for haircuts, nutritional supplements, lessons, automotive repair, food, clothing, babysitting, and books, and we're guessing more that she didn't divulge.

Her blog postings offer up all kinds of handy information about everything from discount shopping to estate sales and dressing on a dime, plus ways to get cool freebies like ice cream, comic books, movie passes, and international phone calls.

Webfloss.com

This is a well-loved site created by Amy Lynn, who describes herself as a Generation X mom, wife, and frugal "live-er." She's skeptical that things can be as good as they seem online. That skepticism benefits readers of her blog because she takes the time to sort out the good and less-good sites to help you live better and for less. Her site is filled with digital treasures, like Daily Deals and Tips Thursday when she posts "random tips" throughout the day about ways to save money, and coupons, and alerts about rip-offs.

You might think buying at a thrift store is pretty basic, but Amy offers really smart advice, which we share here, plus some additional thoughts based on our experience:

- **KNOW YOUR BRANDS.** Amy doesn't bother buying used clothes from discount labels. Instead, she looks for the really good clothing at great prices. Webfloss has lists of popular and high-fashion brands that Amy thinks you should look out for when you're buying secondhand.
- **KNOW SIZES BY INCHES.** With inches, you can be much more certain of getting the right fit, especially for family members who aren't there to try things on. There's a lot of variation in sizes (like waist, inseam, etc.), especially if the item has shrunk. Keep a list of everybody's measurements with you and be sure to update the kids' every few months.
- **TAKE YOUR TIME.** It's easy to snatch up something at a thrift store because it looks cool at the moment and doesn't cost all that much. But we think spending money on almost *anything* without the ability to return it is wasteful. Shopping carefully can save you disappointment as well as dollars. That also translates to checking that zippers, buttons, and snaps are working, and that there are no holes or tears you can't deal with.
- **SHOP WITH A BUDGET AND A LIST.** Think the same way you would if you were shopping retail—with a firm idea of what you're looking for and how much you want to leave at the store.
- **LOOK AROUND.** Some secondhand stores are first rate when it comes to keeping things in order, but others are basically a mess. That means you may find something fantastic on a shelf or in a bin where it doesn't belong. So, the lesson is that you gotta look around.

Freecycle.org

Thrift buyers rave about Freecycle, and it's no wonder. This is a big, busy site made up of thousands of groups that include millions of members worldwide. The grassroots, nonprofit movement, as its creators call it, is all about people giving and getting stuff for free in their local communities, and keeping it out of the trash.

The site was born in 2003 when Deron Beal sent an e-mail announcing The Freecycle Network to a few dozen nonprofit groups in the Tucson area. At the time, Deron was working with a nonprofit recycling group that was trying to find homes for things that other nonprofits no longer needed. Thinking there had to be a better way, he created a Freecycle e-mail group in Tucson that has spread to eighty-five countries and keeps about 500 tons of castoffs out of landfills every day. It's easy to find your local group, post a message, and start giving and getting.

How to Organize Your Own Swap

There's really not that much to planning a swap of books, toys, or kids' clothes. You should definitely try it. Know and do these things first:

- **SPREAD THE WORD.** Choose your date, time, and place, and invite family, friends, neighbors, people from your kids' schools, etc. E-mail is your most efficient and cheapest way to get the word out. Ask people to forward the e-mail appropriately.
- **ESTABLISH GUIDELINES.** For example, "Toys must be clean and in working condition." The guidelines can address size/age for clothing, whether the items should be dropped off or brought to the event, and the entrance free if you're charging one. Some

swappers require a bag of clothes to enter; these can be swapped or given away. Include the guidelines in your e-mail.

- **ORGANIZE AND SET UP.** Keep your tables orderly, with one type of item per table. Make sure there is plenty of room for people to move around. If you're planning an outside swap, have a rain plan.
- **SWAP STRATEGY.** Here's one way to do it, but there are many others. For about the first hour, everyone walks around and looks at the items. Then everyone picks a number and, in order, each participant takes an item. You go around a set number of times, and then it's more or less a free-for-all with people selecting anything else they'd like.
- **HAVE A CLEAN-UP/GIVEAWAY PLAN.** Swappers often arrange for a nonprofit organization to come by at the end of the event to haul away everything that's left.
- **MUNCHIES.** Low-cost snacks and beverages are always welcome, especially if there will be kids in tow.

The possibilities are endless: a mother-and-daughter book swap, a father-and-son toy swap for little and big boys' toys, a casserole or dessert swap (disposable containers and foods that are okay at room temperature are a must), a kitchen equipment swap, a baby furniture swap, and so on.

Yard Sale 101

Evie learned a lot about yard sales from her friend Catherine, who learned all she knew from her friend Stephanie. Traditionally, that's the way we learn about yard sales, and to some degree, it still is. But the Internet has added hugely to the mix by giving people ongoing outlets like Craigslist and Freecycle. With these and other sites, you don't have to wait until Saturday's sales. You can buy and sell 24/7.

But don't think for a minute that yard sales are passé. Some say they're bigger than ever, with literally thousands taking place every weekend. They're fun to have and visit, and you're likely to find a used (and sometimes unused) version of anything you need for your kids, your house, and yourself.

So Many Sales, So Little Time

 From the first Thursday in August through that Sunday, the World's Longest Yardsale takes place along a 654-mile stretch of land from West Unity, Ohio, to Gadsden, Alabama. Also known as the 127 Corridor Sale, it's as much a cultural phenomenon as an opportunity to give and get rid of stuff. And we mean *stuff!* The variety is as vast as you can imagine, with both professional and weekend sellers represented.

Shop for furniture, antiques, coins, clothing, baby things, electronics, collectibles, car gear, and on and on. The culture of the event is renowned. Slow traffic along the route gives people the opportunity to get out and explore the area, including local sights, scenery, riverboats, music, arts, and fishing. After more than twenty years, the event has really become a happening. People come by car, truck, motor home . . . some even fly in! Rooms are booked up to a year in advance. Learn more at 127sale.com.

To learn more about yard sales and how you can get the most out of them, we turned to the Yard Sale Queen—Chris Heiska. Chris runs the website Yardsalequeen.com. (Clever Chris! You can also get there through Garagesalequeen.com.) She also writes a fun and useful blog, Yardsalequeen.blogspot.com, where she introduces herself like this: "I'm Chris, and I am addicted to yard sales, garage sales, thrift stores, and bargain hunting in general."

Chris explained that when she and her husband moved to Lusby, Maryland, she was a "normal" person who shopped in malls. But tiny Lusby is more than an hour from the closest shopping center, and that got Chris to thinking about all those yard sales she saw in the paper.

She started hitting sales on Saturday mornings—and the rest, as they say, is history. Chris decorated the couple's home, and got things for herself and her husband, and by the time their son was born, "yardsaling" (don't dare tell Chris it's not a word) was in her blood. When we talked with Chris, she had recently scored a Wii system for an astounding ten dollars. Okay, it was a Japanese model and had to be retrofitted by Chris's husband, but that's part of the fun, of course.

Chris shared some of her terrific yard sale shopping tips:

- TARGET YOUR MISSION. Newspaper listings aren't enough. Browse everything from flyers posted in the grocery store to the church notes section of the local paper. Once you've identified the sales you want to hit, plan out your route to save time and money. Keep good notes and mark your calendar for recurring events like annual sales you've liked in the past.
- TOOLS OF THE TRADE. Don't come to a sale empty-handed. Chris recommends bringing along a hat/sunglasses, sunscreen, hand sanitizer, a small cooler with beverages, comfy shoes,

small bills and change, and a local map. Keep a few recycled shopping bags in the car so that searching for a bag doesn't slow you down once a hot sale opens, as well as a tape measure and a multi-purpose tool. You might need the scissors to cut a rope to strap something to the car or the small screwdriver to check a battery compartment. Some people even keep various-sized batteries in their car to test battery-operated items.

- **STORE WITH CARE.** Keep a cardboard box or strong tote in the car to hold your stuff. It keeps things from rolling around as you head to the next sale. And it prevents the heartbreak of dropping treasured finds on the way into the house!

- **AIM LOW.** Sometimes sellers have an inflated sense of what their castoffs are worth. Price also depends on when you shop, since by the end of a sale, everyone is ready to get rid of things. Some sellers are simply happy to have an item hauled off so they don't have to store it or bring it back in the house. Many smart shoppers return late in the day to locations they've already scouted to see what's left and at what price.

- **LOOK IT OVER.** When you get home, take a serious look at what you've got. Once Chris bought a set of building toys for her son. When she got home, she discovered some nails and tacks tossed into the canister. Take the time to sort and thoroughly clean everything you bring home, especially a toy for a toddler who will take one look at it and stick it in her mouth.

- **HANG TOUGH.** If you discover a great sale, avoid the temptation to hurry on to the next. A good sale is something to be treasured, and the next one might be a serious disappointment.

- **CONFIRM AND RECONFIRM.** Make sure what you think you're getting is what you're getting. A box for a great, up-to-date printer may not contain that up-to-date printer.

- **KNOW YOUR CUSTOMERS.** Kids' feet grow ridiculously fast. Chris recommends keeping a tracing of their feet attached to cardboard with you so you can safely shop for shoes and boots. If the cardboard foot won't fit into the shoe, it's too small. If it won't lie down, it's too narrow. See where the "toe" ends to assess where there's a little bit of growing room.

- **PRICING POINTERS.** When asking the price of an item, get the seller to name the price rather than ask what you want to pay for it. When you're the seller, try to get the customer to name the price. You can always refuse if it's too low, and if they name a fairly high price, it's gravy. If your kids are with you, have them pay for items themselves. This helps teach them the value of a dollar (especially if they're old enough to compare the five-dollar sneakers with the fifty-dollar sneakers at the mall). And, says Chris, a seller is more likely to offer a good price to a kid clutching a couple of dollars than to a parent with a checkbook. Another note about price: If you see an item you like but it is priced too high, leave your name and number with the seller. You may well hear from them. Some serious sale shoppers bring a laptop and search online for prices to make sure they're getting top value.

- **GET A RECEIPT.** If you purchase a large item, like a sofa or bunk beds, you may have to come back later with a truck to pick it up. Before you leave, Chris advises getting a receipt if you've paid in cash or with a check. Some sellers are leery of checks. When you come back, exchange the check for cash. Also, take a "piece" of the item (like a drawer from a kid's dresser) with you. That prevents someone else from offering more for the item than what you paid.

There are lots more great tips on the Yard Sale Queen's website and blog, including a section on scams and pointers for organizing a sale, such as local regulations, best and worst times of year, and how to advertise. Important note: Your mobile cash register should be a fanny pack that stays with/on you, not a cigar box that's easy to misplace.

Get the Kids Involved

If you do choose to bring the kids along, make sure to keep them close. Items at sales are not secured, and a sale environment could be hazardous.

Whether you're shopping in someone's backyard or at a large urban flea market, the safety of your child should be top of mind at all times. For 25 years, the National Center for Missing & Exploited Children (NCMEC) has been a valuable resource for parents and others who care for and about children.

NCMEC has an excellent set of recommendations to help protect kids while shopping or at other locations. The first step is to talk with your children about safety before heading out, especially in places where there will be crowds and where kids can become separated from Mom or Dad. You need a plan so that you, and your child, will know what to do.

The center says parents should ALWAYS do the following:

- Require children to stay with you at all times at sales or stores.
- Accompany and supervise children in restrooms.
- Establish a pre-designated spot to meet if you become separated. This takes just a minute but should be done every time, every place.
- Teach kids to look for people who can help, like a person in

charge or a mother with children. Of course in malls and stores that can be a uniformed security officer.

The NEVER list includes the following:

- Dress children in clothing that reveals their first or last names. This can attract unwanted attention from someone trying to start a conversation with your child.
- Leave kids at sales or stores and expect that they will be supervised by people in charge.
- Attend a sale or go anywhere with your child if you think you're going to be distracted. If that's the case, ask a friend or neighbor to babysit.
- Drop older children off at sales, thrift stores, etc. without a clear plan for picking them up. The plan should include where, what time, and what to do in case of a change in plans.

There's more essential safety information at the NCMEC website, missingkids.com.

Kids enjoy sales, often more than "real stores," and you're likely to score great toys, books, and clothes for them. Kids love adventure, and a "field trip" to a flea market or yard sale is guaranteed cheap fun. We've got some simple ways to involve the kids. (If your child is going to be whiny and distract you, consider leaving him home with a neighbor; you watch her child later in the day while she goes food shopping.)

- **PLAN YOUR ROUTE TOGETHER.** Get a city map and figure out where you're going and the best route to get there. Your child can be the official trip navigator.

- **BALANCE THAT BUDGET.** Sit down before you hit the sales and crunch the numbers. Explain to your child how much money you have to spend, and what you expect to buy and are looking for. Write this down in a little notebook and keep a running tally of what you've spent and the balance after each purchase. This can be done at a very simple level for a four- or five-year-old, or you can get a little more sophisticated for an older child. Because you can get something for very little at a garage sale, let your child "practice" being a consumer. Give kids a couple of dollars (maybe pulled from a piggy bank or "earned" if this works for you) and put them in control of their own spending.
- **WORK IT, KIDS.** If you're putting on a yard sale, get the kids to help make flyers and signs, price items, make and attach price tags, and run a lemonade stand. We also love the idea of a "free box." Sale shoppers absolutely love this, and it's a great project for the kids. Have them go through their stuff, decide what items are a little more used than others, and recommend them for the free box.
- **DARE TO DE-CLUTTER.** Kids of all ages will be more cheerful about cleaning up their rooms if they can sell unwanted things and keep part of the profits with the approval of Mom and Dad. Help them make decisions about getting rid of electronics, musical instruments, and sports equipment. But give the kids a say-so in smaller stuff they'd like to part with. Encourage them to create little 25-cent grab bags containing a few tiny toys. These can bring real joy to another child.
- **SHARE THE PROFITS.** Some families give a portion of their yard sale profits to a charity or nonprofit. If that's your plan, consider getting the family involved in the decision. Kids of about

ten or so can do Internet research on groups they've heard of. We also like the idea of hand-delivering the profits to the organization if it's local. See if you can get a brief tour, if appropriate. This helps kids understand whom the money they helped earn is going to help. The same is true for household or personal possessions you purchase with money from your sale. If the family worked together to make the sale happen, they'll take more interest and ownership in what you buy with the proceeds. Doing a sale with another family is a fun way to socialize and share duties. One family can be in charge of publicity and signs, while the second family supplies sandwiches and drinks for the workers.

Go Shopping . . . in Your Own Closet

Repurposing helps you look good and save money—two of our main food groups. When you shop in your own closet, that fabulous outfit you admired at the mall last week may not be out of your price range after all. Remember the white blouse that went so beautifully with the charcoal pleated skirt? You gave away the skirt years ago. The blouse is still in style, but you never figured out what else to put with it, so it hasn't been touched in ages!

Everybody gets into a clothes rut. We turn to the same items day after day, but taking a fresh look at our wardrobe can reveal dozens of new possibilities. The first step is to remove everything from the closet. After you've covered the bed, spread out some sheets and arrange items neatly on the floor. Do this by categories—tops, skirts, slacks, jackets, etc. Remove any items that are obviously unwearable because they don't fit, look horrible, and so on.

Then begin to identify new combinations. Put possible outfits together and re-hang them in the closet. Then try on each new combination and see if it works. If it does, hang it neatly in the closet, along with a belt, scarf or other accessory. See if you can wear something "new" from your closet every day for a week! You'll be surprised at all the options at your fingertips.

Make a special pile for soiled, torn or otherwise "fixable" pieces that you'd like to hang onto. Set a goal of getting these back in circulation within a couple of weeks. Take the never-to-be-worn items to the Salvation Army or local shelter, or begin to gather things for a sale.

Kids' clothes are a different story because they grow out of them so quickly. We recommend a periodic (every few months) closet/drawer review and clean-out. Getting items out of the closet that aren't being worn feels great, and it also gives you items to barter, loan, sell, or hand down.

Gifts That Grow in the Garden

We think backyard gardening is one of the best ways in the world to live for less. It's the ultimate example of bartering—you give time and effort, and Mother Nature gives sun and rain. The result is healthful, "free" food you've grown yourself. What's not to love?

Playing in the dirt and getting to eat the results is fun for kids of all ages. Even beginners can do very well at it. Getting started is as easy as planting a couple of tomato and cucumber plants in a nicely tilled sunny spot in the yard (when there's no more danger of frost) and watching them grow. You can keep it that simple, or within a few seasons become quite expert as you learn what grows well in your area, and how to plant, harvest, water, and keep out the creatures. As a family activity, it's got everything going—there are jobs for every age, it *requires* getting dirty, it's an excuse to get outside, and it's physical.

Gardening is also a neat way to help kids relate to the food on their plate, increase their interest in nutrition, and connect with other families. Your family grows and shares tomatoes and peppers, a couple down the street grows enough herbs for the entire neighborhood, and a family with a big backyard contributes lettuce and squash. It's an instant community garden.

There are wonderful gardening websites and books galore on the topic. We have learned a great deal from the Cooperative Extension Services associated with many public universities. A few tips for starting a garden:

- **CRAWL BEFORE YOU WALK.** Start with a small space that won't be overwhelming for you or your child. Kids can really do every aspect of gardening. Tilling may seem like grown-up work, but give a three-year-old a big spoon and a few feet of earth, and you'll be amazed at how much soil can be overturned.

- **BE CREATIVE WITH CONTAINERS.** If you live in an apartment or townhome, consider container gardening on your patio or balcony. Vegetables like lettuce, Swiss chard, tomatoes, and beans can do very well in containers.

- **NURTURE NURTURING.** Planting is fun, but watering and weeding may not be as exciting. Help the kids become responsible by creating a gardening calendar that tells them on which days they should water. Put stickers on the days they've done their chores.

- **CONSIDER A PIZZA GARDEN.** Plant in a circle divided into wedge shapes. Each child is responsible for one of the wedges, with different plants in each. A pizza garden can also be a combination of veggies and herbs that you actually put on a pizza, like tomatoes, peppers, basil, and chives.

- **SIZE IT RIGHT.** Kids do much better with tasks if their tools are right-sized. Invest in a child-sized rake, hoe, spade, and gloves.

It's pretty easy to keep the interest in gardening alive over the winter months by inside gardening. Here's how:

- **SPROUT ROOTS.** Place any type of bean seeds on paper towels and put them close to a window in plastic cups or zipper bags. You don't even need dirt. Just keep them moist with a spray bottle. The roots will sprout and grow in no time.
- **PLANT "POT PEOPLE."** Decorate terra cotta or other pots with faces. (Make sure they have a drainage hole.) Fill them with soil and add grass seed, topped with a light layer of soil. Water with a spray bottle and place near a window. The grass makes funky hair for your plant pot person that's fun to trim when it gets too long.
- **WE DIG AVOCADOES.** The next time you have a couple of avocado pits left over from making guacamole, let the kids turn them into plants. Rinse the pit well and dry it. Push a few toothpicks into the pit so the upper part is dry and the lower part is suspended in a cup with about an inch of water. Put the plant on a bright windowsill. In about three to six weeks, a sprout will appear from the top, and roots will grow from the bottom. At this point, you can transplant your avocado "tree" into a large pot filled with soil, with about half the plant above the soil line. In a few years, you may even get fruit.

Planting and harvesting aren't the only things to do in your garden. It's a place to play and learn in ways like these:

- **READ.** Take out library books about gardens, plants, nature, etc., spread out a blanket in or near the garden, and read. Read to one another or enjoy peaceful "parallel" time when you and your child read separately.
- **JOURNAL.** Assign an interested child the job of making and keeping a garden journal. Encourage her to note what was planted when and where, when blooms and vegetables appeared, etc. This becomes your road map for next year's planting. A picture journal is perfect for pre-schoolers.
- **COOK YOUR HARVEST.** It's such fun to cook what you grow. And produce offers a natural way to get your child interested in all those good-for-you foods.
- **DISCOVER.** Learn about the role of bees and other creatures in the growing process.

Thoughts About Safety

When you're buying secondhand items, especially for children, you want to be really careful about the condition of the things you bring home. Find out from the seller if you can return the item if it's not working or seems unsafe. And if you're on the selling side, we recommend checking on your own items to make sure they haven't been recalled. It's easy to do by going to the website of the U.S. Consumer Product Safety Commission at CPSC.gov. You don't want to buy or sell a recalled crib or a toy that's been found to be a choking hazard!

We also want you to think about safety in financial terms. If you're swapping or bartering for business-oriented services, there might be tax implications to consider. Be sure to ask a tax professional if you have questions.

Next, get ready to celebrate while you create terrific memories for your family. Chapter 6 is all about parties—better, more fun, and more meaningful on any budget.

6

The Party Circuit— Simpler, Sweeter, Cheaper

NOD IF YOU SPEND HOURS planning and preparing for your child's birthday parties. Nod if you've found yourself swept up in birthday party madness. All that nodding tells us that you could use some fresh ideas to make your parties long on fun and meaning, even if you're short on funds.

You can stop nodding. But don't stop reading because this chapter is a celebration of parties, with sweet, fun ideas that are less about keeping up with the Joneses and more about keeping your head and heart in the right place.

As your kids' Chief Memory Officer, it's useful to stop and think about what makes a party great. Think back on a party you attended as a child—yours or somebody else's. What do you remember? If it was your party, you probably best remember the gifts. But what about other kids' celebrations?

We pooled our memories and came up with a pretty predictable list. Evie remembers playing outdoor games like Red Rover, and Robyn remembers the colorful decorations. They both recall favorite cakes their moms made. Robyn's was a choo-choo circus train with animals in every car, and Evie's was a gorgeous ballerina. We both remember the excitement of bringing home a little goody bag with some candy "for later." Sweet memories, indeed.

The point is, it's just not about elaborate activities or choreographed entertainment. Too much planned stuff can actually make kids anxious. They want to run around, play some games, and eat yummy treats without being over-programmed. And, of course, politely deliver their "thank-yous" when it's all over. Even if it's simple, a party should be well-planned to cover all the things that matter most to you, including keeping kids safe and engaged.

The biggest thing to keep in mind in planning a party that's memorable and affordable is whose party it is (your child's or her friends'), and whose party it isn't (yours). In Robyn's book *Make It Memorable: An A-to-Z Guide to Making Any Event, Gift or Occasion . . . Dazzling* she stresses the importance of thinking about the birthday child's interests and an age-appropriate activity kids can actually do and enjoy.

Trust us, you don't need to truck in snow for sledding or hire a Disney character to hand-deliver invitations to your guests. We've got super creative ideas that are excessively fun, without the excess. These ideas will have your little guests (and their parents) wondering what's next and how you came up with so many touches they've never seen before. Keep things real with kid-made invites, hilarious new games, and easy, no-fail treats.

Rules of the Party-Planning Game

- **SHORT AND SWEET.** How long should you party? An hour and a half max for kids under three (any younger, and you might just stick with cake and ice cream with the family and grandparents) and no more than two hours for those under six.
- **NUMBERS COUNT.** In a perfect world, an eight-year-old gets to have nine guests (one for each year plus herself). But things can get complicated when there are rules or expectations about inviting everyone in a child's class. One side of the argument says life isn't fair, and everybody doesn't get invited to everything, no matter what the age. The other side says it's bad form and snarky to exclude any member of a class or play group. The decision is up to you, and we lean toward no hurt feelings. If you're going to end up with lots of kids, consider teaming up with a child with a close birthday and sharing the party. This can be great fun and, in some families, becomes a happy tradition.
- **CALL FOR HELP.** Any time you've got more than a couple of kids in a room, you need a helper. Deputize a grandparent or friend who can do whatever needs to be done—escort little ones to the bathroom, take photos and video, pass out the little ice cream cups, etc. This is no time for martyrdom; you are definitely going to need another set of hands!

A Word About Where

We're all in favor of home parties and affordable venues, but we know it's easy to overdo it. Bottom line—you don't want to be paying for a child's party for weeks or months! Miniature golf, bowling, and other venues can get expensive, especially when the "party package" rate is double-digit-dollars per child.

Keep your eye out for specials that could make these fun venues more affordable. For example, if you see a coupon for the skating rink in the paper, you can feel confident that they are looking for business. Call and ask if they're offering any unpublicized group or party specials. Sometimes, you can really score a great deal this way.

Keep your expectations and those of your child reasonable. Don't promise a movie theater party until you've figured out that it is possible and within your budget. No question, birthdays are absolutely huge for kids, as they should be. But it's just not smart to over-promise. Kids are perfectly able to handle, "Let's see what we can figure out."

It's such fun to say yes that we sometimes forget about the "joys" of saying no. Your child learns that all things are not possible and is able to handle disappointments. That's its own gift.

Create a Schedule

Assume nothing, plan everything in advance, and anticipate that your orderly party schedule will be subject to all kinds of potential disruptions and changes. From the moment kids arrive to that happy wave good-bye, the goal is to keep things moving according to a plan you've created in advance, but one that's certain to change. There's no value in overly micromanaging this—it's a kids' party. But for your peace of mind and the children's enjoyment, know where you're heading.

There will be fewer meltdowns if you've got more things planned than you have time for. That way, you can stick with a game or activity that's working really well without fear that you'll run out of activities. And if you do? No big deal. Head to your downstairs playroom or safe, supervised yard and let things take their kidly course.

Here's how a schedule might look for an hour-and-a-half party. It's basically the same whether you have invited the adults to stay or not. That's another one of those personal decisions, but we think that after about age five, kids are better off without the parents hovering around. Generally speaking, if your child is old enough for a drop-off play date, she's old enough to attend a party without you.

Sample party schedule

- **2:00 PM:** Plan for kids arriving early. For example, set out a big roll of craft paper and crayons or markers at a kid-size table. Designate a place where guests can leave jackets and belongings and a table or large bag for presents.
- **2:10 PM:** As the guests arrive, lead them to a name-tag table where they can make and decorate a colorful name tag. This is essential if you're going to be in a public place, but it's also nice to do at home in case children don't know one another and so that adults in charge can call the kids by name.
- **2:20 PM:** Primary game or activity (see lots of ideas below) begins. Allow a few minutes at the beginning to get rolling and at the end to wrap up whatever you're doing. This isn't boot camp. On the other hand, you want to keep things fun and feeling good.
- **3:00 PM:** The activity ends, and kids gather around the table for party food and cake. We like the idea of a mini-activity while they're getting seated and you're opening the ice-cream cups, lighting the candles, etc. Depending on the age, this could be really simple like leading a couple of familiar songs.

Or ask a capable older friend or sibling to perform a couple of magic tricks or tell some age-appropriate jokes. Then it's time for candles, cake, singing "Happy Birthday," and serving. As the kids are eating, you might want to go around the table (this works best when it's a small group with talkative kids!) and have each guest say something about the birthday child—how they got to know him and what they like to do together. Or have each guest tell his or her own birthday; even the most shy kids love to do this.

- **3:30 PM:** The party ends, and guests are given a party favor as they leave. If the parents have not been invited, they come in, pick up their children, and escort them out.

Speaking of Mom and Dad, if they are invited, make sure you've got a place for them to put their belongings. Hopefully, they'll enjoy the scene while staying in the background. Parents love to help. Hand out a few disposable cameras and let them click away. Or ask each parent to bring a camera and e-mail you the photographs. A special snack or dessert table for the adults is a nice touch. No hot beverages, please!

Keeping It Priceless

When your child is young, parties are small and easy to oversee. As kids start school and make friends from their classroom and activities, the list grows. Once your child is on the party circuit, the pressure can mount. So what do you do if you find yourself in a group or community where parents seem to be trying to outdo one another's parties? Same rule applies: Remember whose party it is (your child's and her friends'), and whose party it isn't (yours).

Don't be afraid to break the pattern and do something fresher and more memorable. We've done it, and we know it works. More fun. More creative. More "this is what we can afford" and less "this is what everybody's doing."

For example, everybody's had the experience of opening up a big toy and discovering that the kids love the box more than whatever they were supposed to love inside it. Presto. Transform a corrugated carton into a pretend house, fort, or castle. One couple we know scored six large boxes from a furniture supply store in advance of their son Ethan's birthday party.

They checked them over carefully to make sure they were clean, with no staples, nails, or other potential hazards. With the help of Ethan and his siblings, the couple minimally decorated the boxes, painting a few doors and windows, smiley faces, trees, and birthday graffiti on them. Then, on party day, they filled their backyard with the boxes and put some dress-up clothes in them.

The two- and three-year-olds had a blast pretending their hearts out and running in and out of what they called Ethan's Fun City! The boxes were such a hit that Mom and Dad left a couple of them in the family's playroom where they were enjoyed until they fell apart.

Another break-the-mold party idea is a mini fair or festival with "stations" staffed by grandparents and friends. This is easy to adapt for kids of different ages. Robyn did this for Ali's fourth party, and it was dynamite. Ideas for stations are endless—decorating tiny pumpkins or sugar cookies, face painting, making a clay craft, paper folding, seed planting, manicures, hair-dos, and making greeting cards.

Other Ways to Save

There are lots of ways to save on the party you choose. One is to team up with a family whose son or daughter has a birthday near your child's. Of course, this really only works if the children share friends through school or activities. Evie got together with another family to put on a fun surprise pool party for Erica and her friend Ryan. Because they had more or less the same friends, the price of everything was cut in half. Some others we've tried and recommend:

Piggyback the party

Cut the expense, maybe even in half, by piggybacking a party with another event. When Ali turned one, Robyn planned a party that celebrated her grandmother Pauline's big eightieth birthday and Ali's little one. This was perfect because a party for a one-year-old really turns into an adult/family party anyway, which was exactly what everybody wanted. Grandma Pauline got a big cake, and Ali got a tiny one.

It was totally memorable, and the older folks loved connecting with the babies. The photos were fabulous and made great family gifts at the holidays.

Locations for less

The most affordable place to have a party is usually at your home or in a public park. But if those aren't going to work, get creative. Find out about available community spaces—a party room at your local library, an environmental preserve, a beach shelter, or even a family member's large finished basement.

Make it yourself

If you're serving lunch or an early supper, it's tempting to bring in pizza, fast-food kid meals, and the like. But making the food at home will save you a bunch of money. It also lets you control the ingredients, feeding your guests what you'd want your own kids to eat. Pizza dough costs pennies. Stretch it, top it, and bake it (you can do all of this ahead and freeze the shells) for a yummy meal that guests of all ages will love.

Making personal pizzas can also be your party activity. Fill plastic bowls with favorite toppings. Each guest gets an aluminum pie pan with his or her name on the bottom in permanent marker and an orange-sized piece of dough. Have a couple of jars of sauce available and grown-up assistance as needed. The kids will love stretching the dough, ladling out sauce, and applying cheese and toppings. Add to the fun by having the kids decorate and wear their own paper chefs' hats. Make sure hands are scrubbed before and after cooking, of course! You can also use flatbread or small pitas to make pint-sized pizzas.

You can bake off quite a few of these at the same time using two or three oven racks and switching them in the middle of the 15-minute baking time (450 degrees F). Your best bet is to have one adult in charge of baking and slicing each finished pie into four pieces and delivering them to the table.

Also fun is a make-your-own sandwich bar for ages six and up. (Kids much younger don't really eat sandwiches, but they do like bite-size finger foods.) Or let the party-goers dress their own dogs. Boil or grill hot dogs (be mindful of what's in them, please!) and have lots of toppings to choose from. This is as messy as it is yummy, so consider doing it outside on a couple of picnic tables.

Other affordable party foods we like include Sloppy Joes on hamburger buns (search online for an easy recipe), a pot of not-spicy chili in cooler weather (make it ahead and it's even better), homemade chicken nuggets, or cheesy lasagna.

Let Them Have . . . Cake!

Trust us when we say you do *not* have to be a master baker to pull off a "Mom-you're-the-best" birthday cake. If the idea of creaming butter and sugar causes your pulse to rise, start with a good quality cake mix. It's one of those times when we endorse processed food!

Buy mixes when they're two-for-one and store them. They have a shelf life of about a million years, so you don't have to worry about that part! Store-bought cakes are easy to buy and reasonably priced, but there's something about doing it at home that creates the best memories.

There are some awesome websites that show you step-by-step how to decorate fabulous cakes, from Evie's ballerina-in-the-center and Robyn's circus train to a cake decorated like Dora or Pooh Bear. Check websites like coolest-birthday-cakes.com; it's a lot less intimidating and a lot more fun than you might think. If the whole decorating thing is too much, keep it simple with a rectangular cake (maybe two or three cake mixes large depending on the number of guests) and personalize it with miniature toys or objects that are all about the birthday child.

You can also make the cake part of the party activity. Decorating cupcakes is a guaranteed sloppy success with kids of any age. Bake them un-iced in advance (they freeze beautifully) and let the children frost and decorate with toppings like M&Ms, licorice pieces, gumdrops or any candy that's age-appropriate and easy to manipulate. Do not, we repeat, do *not* attempt to send cupcakes home, no matter how clever the little holder you dream up. This won't work and is a guaranteed mess and parent displeaser.

If you'd rather buy than make, go for it! It's so okay to fake it and not bake it. In fact, we love the idea of using a store-bought iced cake and adding your personal touch to give it the look of a from-scratch masterpiece.

Faker baker cakes

- **PEPPERMINT CAKE.** Crush peppermint sticks and sprinkle over a frosted cake, especially during the holidays. You get a yummy mint flavor and a colorful crunch.
- **CANDY-BAR CAKE.** Buy a few of your child's favorite candy bars. Slice them into bite-sized slivers and decorate the edge of the cake with the pieces. Or slice the cake horizontally through the center, top with pudding and candy bar pieces, and put the cake back together to create a delicious surprise layer.
- **CHARACTER CAKES.** Use clean, plastic figures (with no loose pieces that could break off) to create a cake topper. Most anything can go on top of a cake as long as it's easily removed and doesn't sink into the icing. Insert a small, iced plastic lid to hold a character or toy and prevent it from sinking in or being ruined by the icing.
- **YUCKY CAKE.** Decorate with lots of gummy worms and other yucky-looking candies like chocolate ladybugs. You might have to go to a candy store to get these, but they are so worth it. Stick to soft candies that are easy to chew.
- *BEAN* **THERE, DONE THIS.** Spell out your child's name and age in jelly beans and M&Ms. We also love to decorate an entire cake—top and trim—with M&Ms.

- **SPLATTER CAKE.** This is really fun to do. Get small tubes of icing in different colors and let your child squeeze it all over an iced cake. Think Jackson Pollock and create a masterpiece that will be a centerpiece sensation.
- **PICTURE THIS.** Personalize your cake by adding photographs that have been laminated or attached to Popsicle sticks.
- **GO FISH!** Use small Goldfish crackers to create a neat-looking school of fish. Looks great on top of blue frosting!
- **CHIP OFF THE OL' BLOCK.** Sprinkle mini chocolate chips over the iced cake. It's a great look and adds flavor and crunch. Do the same with colored sprinkles and confetti found in the cake-decorating aisle of the grocery store.
- **POLKA DOTS.** This one hits the spot. Take a small, round, flat cookie or candy and gently press into the icing to create a happy-looking cake.

Theme It Up

Themes are great and can really help enhance a party, as long as they don't get out of control. If you're going to do a theme, make the main party activity the payoff if possible. If the theme is soccer, involve everybody in a fun soccer game. If the theme is art, bring in an artistic friend to teach ten-year-olds how to do caricatures that they can take home as their party favor.

Check out these awesome themes:

- **BEACH PARTY.** Come in your swimsuit and, weather permitting, splash in sprinklers or wading pools. Older kids can play "beach" volleyball.
- **CANDY LAND.** Create crafts with candy and play the classic game.

- **PIRATES PARTY.** Plan a treasure hunt with plenty of booty to be found.
- **SECRET GARDEN.** Create a mini take-home garden with cups or egg cartons and seeds.
- **HAT PARTY.** Get inexpensive hats or caps from the dollar store, decorate them with fabric, craft remnants and markers, and hold a hat fashion show when the parents arrive to pick up the kids. (Tell them to come fifteen minutes early with cameras in hand.)
- **BACKWARD PARTY.** Old-school fun—wear clothing and shoes backward. Say good-bye when everyone arrives!
- **CRAFT PARTY.** Get the makings for jewelry or painted ceramics, or create junk sculptures from stuff you've collected ahead of time.
- **MAD SCIENTIST.** Get the kids involved in a fun science experiment like making a volcano or a simple homemade radio. Do your homework on this one and choose a project that's super safe.
- **HOLIDAY PARTIES.** If your child's birthday is close to a holiday, you've got an instant theme. For example, a Halloween party is always fun. Games like passing around a tray of scary foods in the dark (peeled grapes for eyeballs, cold spaghetti for guts) are always a hit. If your party is near the winter holidays, consider a give-back component like asking guests to bring an outgrown sweater, umbrella, or book that you collect and distribute to kids in need.
- **DANCE PARTY.** This can be such fun, especially if you go retro with a '50s or '60s theme and costumes. Have someone teach a real jitterbug, include a dance contest, and serve mini burgers and shakes.

- **CHEF PARTY.** Make your own ice cream, cupcakes, or trail mix. Everyone gets an apron to decorate and take home. Channel your child's *Top Chef.*
- **OLYMPICS PARTY.** This is such a neat idea, especially when the party is close to the "real" Olympics. Come up with your own Olympic sports, like three-legged races and crazy relays. If you can't find "medals" at the dollar store, ask friends who run in races to contribute those race medals they're sure to have around.
- **KARAOKE.** If your child is an aspiring singer, a karaoke party can be a blast. You can turn your speakers into a karaoke machine if you're just the slightest bit handy. Search this process on YouTube or Google. It's a great way to get the fun of karaoke without renting an expensive set.

Could It Get Any Simpler?

We're not sure why parties get so stale and repetitive when there are so many fun, simple things you can do. Help your child have a "ball" on her birthday by building an entire party around balls. Get a bunch of balls (big red rubber balls, beach balls, jacks and balls, etc.) at the dollar store or the big-box store when they're on sale. A ball becomes each child's take-home favor, but they're also used for organized activities during the party. Play basketball games like HORSE spelled with the birthday child's name. Play Follow the Leader with a ball. Set up Musical Chairs in which kids walk around while the music is playing, and then when the music stops, they have to grab a ball and sit on it. Of course, there's one fewer than the number of players each round.

There's always dodge ball or, depending on the weather and access to a court or field, you can host a softball or T-ball party. The team uniform is a colored cap from the dollar store. Decorate these in advance with the name of the birthday child and the date, and hand them out as you divide the kids into teams. (This theme's a natural for snacks like hot dogs and Cracker Jack, which you can totally make at home, then bag up and add a little toy.)

Don't forget classic fun like blowing bubbles (outside, thanks very much). Every child gets a bottle of bubbles. (Have plenty of homemade replacement solution ready—⅔ cup dishwashing soap, 1 gallon water, and 2–3 tablespoons glycerin, available at your pharmacy.) Take pictures and e-mail them to the parents as a way of thanking your guests for coming and showing off some of the hugest bubbles.

Got a special friend or family member whose generosity you could count on to create a really unique party? Maybe you know someone who owns a farm and could host a hayride. Perhaps your neighbor works at a small airport and could give the kids a cool tour of the facility. Evie's favorite baby-sitter was a young neighbor who was studying to be a hairdresser. She and a friend did hairstyles for Erica's eleven-year-old party, and the kids absolutely loved it.

There's always the classic outing to the local fire station. When Justin Spizman had a fire-station party, they brought gifts for the firefighters and celebrated these amazing heroes. The kids got to climb on the fire engine, too. Dice the Dalmatian, the Spizmans' dog, was the perfect party mascot.

Check out any free, age-appropriate museums or special exhibits. Sometimes, smaller towns have great little history, transportation, or natural history museums with treasures like stuffed bears and giant snake skins. These can be the focus of an exciting, affordable party outing. If the space and weather permit, combine a visit with a picnic lunch, and you've created a lovely little event.

The Wee Ones

How much party does a one-year-old really need? A first birthday is one of life's greatest moments, especially for parents and grandparents. But the child, in every way still a baby, is simply not going to know or care about a showy party. The key is to create a celebration that allows everyone to really relax and enjoy watching your baby's delight as she digs into her mini-cake face first (if you dare!). Invite some family members and a few friends, arrange some simple snacks, lay out some clean blankets and sanitized toys for tiny guests, and you're there.

Make sure there are plenty of cameras on hand. Ask everyone who's taken pictures that day to send them to you. Create a digital photo album online in minutes and have memories for years. You might also like to take a photo of the baby with each guest as a special keepsake.

By about age two, children love to dress up. Letting them enjoy clothing items and safe "props" like vests, boas, and hats make a perfect party activity for toddlers. Don't forget to take pictures of the little ones in their costumes. If you have a home printer or an instant camera, you can send guests home with pictures.

Making sock or paper-bag puppets is just as fun as you remember and makes a neat party activity/favor. You can also enlist older kids to produce a puppet show to entertain the party-goers.

Treasure hunts are guaranteed fun if you have a park or backyard where you can hide the treasures. It's easy to cut up pages of stickers, and you can find bulk candy and tiny toys for very little money. It's also fun to sprinkle a dollar's worth of pennies around that the kids are quite excited to find. This is really fun to do with older kids, too. Make it harder by using clues to send the kids from find to find.

A storybook party is a sweet idea, even for guests who can't read! Everyone brings a favorite book for swapping. Kids come dressed as the character in their book or as any favorite storybook character. Build the party around the birthday child's favorite storybook and character. Create decorations, a cake, and games to bring the story to life. If you're handy with a needle and thread, create a costume that an adult or teen can wear while reading or acting out a story. They'll love it, especially when the mask or headpiece comes off and a familiar mom or dad appears.

Another simple idea for the little one is an animal party. Boxes of animal crackers are the favors, and the game can be Pin the Tail on Whatever (print big animal images easily from your computer). Or help the kids create animal-ear headbands and have a fun parade around the yard or cul-de-sac. Another fun one is a Color Party. Use lots of rainbow decorations, and let the kids have at it with sidewalk chalk and washable paint or markers on rolled craft paper.

Create a Tradition

Birthday traditions are really special, and the possibilities are limitless. Think about an all-family photo taken in the same location each year, burning down a year on one of those pillar birthday candles, or marking the children's height on the garage door.

Here are a few others:

- A family picnic or bike ride.
- The classic birthday dinner. (As the child gets older, he or she gets to choose the menu.)
- Make-and-take-a-cake to a worthwhile cause or children's shelter to help your child see her birthday as an opportunity to

count and share her blessings.

- Establish roots. Link your child to the natural world by planting a tree in his honor on every birthday.
- Give a small but memorable gift the child can get each year and collect, like a snow dome from a place you visit, a classic book, a copy of that year's *Old Farmer's Almanac*, or a little charm for a bracelet.
- Choose a fun (or silly) family birthday hat that everybody wears on their birthday. The photos are priceless, especially as you see the child age in the same hat.

Inviting Invitations

It's easy to create inexpensive invitations that announce from the get-go that your party will be uniquely creative. Think simple and, with a little shopping know-how, you can find great buys, papers, postcards, and more. Here are some simple ways to save money when creating and sending invitations:

- Make an invitation that matches your theme, like used game tickets for a sports party or a pretend menu for a cooking party. Work with your child to create a poem, limerick, or riddle that conveys the who, what, where, when, and why. Design it on the page, print it out, and stick it in an envelope. From age three, your child can participate in this process, including selecting online graphics or coloring the paper invites after they've been printed.
- If the entire class is invited, don't waste money on postage. Just clear it with the teacher first and distribute them at school. Ask the teacher to send an e-mail that will flag the parents to look

for the invite at the bottom of their child's book bag. Also, postcards cost less to send and are easy to make. For example, you can print the information on a large sticker, and then attach it to a piece of sturdy, recycled cardboard. Check the dimensions on the United States Post Office website (USPS.com) to confirm that the size of your card can go out at current postcard rates.

• Brown bag envelopes are charming and low-key. Get the family involved in transforming ordinary brown lunch bags into extraordinary envelopes. Insert your homemade invite into the bag, fold over a few times, and add a sticker to your "envelope." You can get a little cutesy with the message like, "The cat's out of the bag, and it's Jason's birthday!" Or, "We're having a surprise party for Chloe . . . don't let the cat out of the bag!" Again, check with the USPS website or your local post office to see how much postage is required.

The Scoop on Goody Bags

Everybody looks forward to party favors or goody bags. It's the signature and farewell thank-you for parties. When the party activity becomes the take-home favor, it's a two-in-one deal. Each guest has something by which to remember the party and is thanked for coming. Keep it age-appropriate with affordable items suitable for that age group. Here are some ideas:

• Consider giving something useful that kids will enjoy, like magic markers, crayons, or something art-related you find on a great sale or at the dollar store. Put the art stuff in a lunch bag decorated by the birthday child. Add the child's first name with

the marker and put balls (small circles filled in) on the beginning and ending of each part of the alphabet letter.

- If you love to bake, make and wrap a few sturdy homemade
cookies (like oatmeal raisin) in cellophane and add curled ribbon to each little packet. Check out the website called www.
bakerella.com for clever ideas for baking up yummy creations.
You'll look like a pro when you bake these innovative goodies.

- Kids love tiny stuff, which is, by design, what goes into a goody
bag. Think mini vehicles, lip gloss, a neat little drinking cup or
water bottle, mini coloring books, a tiny notebook and markers or cool pens, small flashlight, something you personalize
like a white baseball cap, or snacks like homemade popcorn
balls or packs of cheese crackers. Allergies and dietary restric-
tions notwithstanding, we're also not averse to a little bag of
candy. It's a birthday, right?

How Do You Feel on Saturday Night?

How do you know if you've done a good job hosting your child's
birthday party? You do it the same way you assess a lot of things
about parenting: by observing your kids. That doesn't mean nobody
has a post-party meltdown; birthdays can get a little crazy, and we
all know that.

We're talking about watching your child during the party. Quiet
or gregarious, was she acting like herself? Was she relaxed and really
having fun? And what about the other children? Were they into the
activity and excited about the games?

We postmodern parents want to do so much for our kids that
sometimes we do a little too much. We complicate and control,
sometimes out of guilt, sometimes out of not knowing what else to

do. A party is an unusual but valuable barometer of your parenting.

Was your child delighted? Was it fun and relatively stress-free for you to do? Did you keep the spending in the comfortable range? Did you help your child move beyond the me-me-me aspect of the birthday to enjoy sharing it with others and maybe even reaching out to someone less fortunate? Did you feel really satisfied on Saturday night, long after the last goody bag was spilled on the driveway? That's the feeling you want to create and repeat next year.

The party's over, but the celebration continues as we enter the glorious world of gifts. Stuck in a present-giving rut? We'll have you unstuck in no time. Turn the page, and let's get started.

7

Low-Cost to No-Cost Gifts

WHAT DO YOU GET WHEN you multiply two birthday parties in one weekend times two or three kids? An empty wallet, that's what! We say cut the cost, but don't spare the sentiment with great ideas you'll find in this chapter. Celebrate birthdays, the holidays, and Mother's and Father's Day with intangible and creative gifts that will be long remembered—not for what you spent, but for what you gave.

Sure, there will be times when you will purchase gifts. But creating unique, personal presents is totally doable even if you're not the craftiest person around. You don't have to be an artist to be a gifted giver *and* save money. You have to know your recipients and what makes them tick.

You're in luck. Robyn is a leading expert on gift giving, and her ideas are frequently sought out by national media. She's also the creator of The Giftionary (TheGiftionary.com), an A-to-Z galaxy of gift giving and an online sponsored gift guide and resource for discovering gifts for all budgets, including gifts that are made by artists all over the country, stay at home moms, and more. Like a dictionary is to words, TheGiftionary.com is to gifts. She has also reported for over three decades about ways to make gift giving more memorable and meaningful. Robyn's valuable and easy to apply premise is to add a piece of yourself to any gift. By making it, baking it, building it, or somehow getting involved in its creation, you show your very personal appreciation for someone else. Maybe you personalize with a paint pen or teach your young children to make a sweet, homemade gift card.

Add the "Ta-Dah Touch"

Making gifts can be a lovely, productive way to spend time with children. We'll show you how to wrap a *so-so* gift and, with just the right touch, transform it into something truly *ta-dah*. And we'll give you the confidence to take a basic skill like photography and use it to create unique presents that feel like a work of art.

"Ta-dah" is a lot of things, including the skill of making gifts appear when you need them. Perhaps you have some unfinished birdhouses in the garage. Have a painting party with your child and put them away in a gift closet. Fill that closet with great finds on books or games so that you're ready at a moment's notice when an invitation comes in. It's incredibly stress-reducing to have gifts at the ready!

We've seen firsthand that when children see parents take the time and effort to personalize a gift, they understand that there are many ways to say thanks, happy birthday, or congratulations. This chapter is jam-packed with bright ideas for gifts that are memorable, magical, and budget friendly.

It's Always Time to Give

What's the right occasion for a gift? Almost any. There are so many reasons to give. You don't need a Hallmark occasion or a calendar event. Sometimes, the most memorable gifts express appreciation or simply remind someone they're tops in your book. What's the right gift? One that comes from your heart and touches the heart of the receiver.

When it comes to presents, Robyn urges you to think outside the gift box. A present can be words on a page, like a beautifully written thank-you note or a funny, personalized limerick or a child's name enlarged and framed. We know one mom who uses a stencil with her child to draw a friend's name in a simple outline with a black marker. The child then fills in the letters with drawings, words, and fun memories they shared.

Sometimes, it's a bit of a hunt to find a gift that is absolutely unique and meaningful. When Justin first learned to use a camera at age six, he took nature photographs at his aunt's beach house. To thank Aunt Lois for a wonderful visit, he photographed a beautiful butterfly that had lighted on a bush in the backyard. They left the photograph at the house framed so Aunt Lois would find it upon her return and even made one for Grandma Phyllis. Another time, he captured an image of a bunny rabbit. To this day, those framed photos are remembered with love and everyone has copies they've enjoyed over the years.

Giving Is the Gift

Gift giving with children can be experiential, like a long walk together on the beach. Collect shells in a treasure box, adding one each summer. Write the date on the bottom with a permanent marker. A gift can be an offering from nature, like a fat summer tomato snipped off the vine or a cutting from a favorite perennial. When a cousin gifted Grandma Phyllis Freedman with a begonia plant more than forty years ago, it led to her becoming an expert begonia grower. Recently, she gave her grandson's fiancée a cutting. Now Jaime is continuing the tradition, and her begonia plant is flourishing and makes Jaime look as if she has a very green thumb!

Here's a list of gift-giving occasions and special events—opportunities to share your appreciation, love, and gratitude. It's just a start. Give when your heart says it's time.

- Get well
- Thanks
- Congratulations
- Thinking of you
- Sad news (food gifts are especially welcome)
- Birthdays
- Anniversaries of all kinds
- Appreciation (teacher, boss, friend, trainer, spouse, customer, etc.)
- Special firsts (lost tooth, sleepover, bike ride without training wheels)
- Last day of school
- Welcomes and farewells
- Milestones (double-digit birthday, new home)
- Graduations (from pre-school on up)

- Achievements (new job, scoring the winning goal, launching a blog, losing ten pounds)
- Assistance with a special need (moving, setting up a computer, entertaining the in-laws, helping your child through a tough moment)

There are lots of helping people in life whose birthday you may never know or celebrate, but whom you may wish to gift for special kindnesses, like a Scout leader, tutor, health-care provider, employee, co-worker or service provider. And that's just the beginning. Being known as a giving person is one of life's great pleasures. Teaching that to your kids is right up there, too.

Untouchable Treasures

So many fabulous gifts can't be wrapped, or even touched for that matter. We had the honor to work on a very special book with Edie Fraser. Its title is *Do Your Giving While You Are Living*. It tells the stories of dozens of remarkable people who have made the decision that sharing their time, talent, and treasure today is what matters most in life. From them we learned about selfless expressions by people who feel incomplete unless they are giving and sharing of themselves.

But here's the good news: You don't have to be the subject of a book to give of yourself and encourage your children to do the same. Here's what we mean:

Give of your time

There is no more meaningful gift than time because it is the most personal and finite commodity. No matter how successful or lucky you are, you are never going to have more than twenty-four hours

(1,440 quick minutes) in every day. Giving your children your undivided attention when they talk about their school day or a scuffle on the playground is a gift.

That means stopping what you're doing—no cell phone or Blackberry in hand—getting down on their level, and listening with all you've got. When you take time to hear out a friend who needs to unload about a messy issue at work, your silent support is a gift. Visiting an ailing aunt or spending time at a nursing home with a total stranger is a gift that will be remembered long after a "thing" is used or tossed.

We're so used to buying that it can take some effort to rethink how and what we give. What can you do? Start to brainstorm around the dinner table about some of the endless ways you and others in the family can give of their time. The possibilities are only limited by your imagination and the needs of those around you. One Sunday, Robyn and her family headed over to the home of an elderly neighbor with rakes in hand. The goal was to rid the lawn of a huge blanket of fall leaves. In raking and bagging the leaves, the Spizmans gave generously of their time to someone who was burdened by the need to get this task done but could no longer make it happen herself.

"We all got in on the act, and it was such a pleasure seeing the look on the face of this elderly widow as she looked out at her yard, wistfully remembering the days when her late husband had kept it spotless. It was a joy to see how appreciative she was. The other benefit was for the children—no, for all of us—to sense that a pretty simple act on our part could mean so much to someone else. It only took us a few hours, and we enjoyed every minute of it."

When floods deluged the small city of Albany, Georgia, Evie and her daughter Erica headed south from Atlanta to join dozens of other volunteers who spent days squeegeeing water and mud out of people's living rooms. They will never forget the experience of working side by side with homeowners who had lost so much. There wasn't much celebrating going on, but the gifts were in evidence for all to see.

Give of your talents

Are you a good cook? Are you a wiz at hanging wallpaper? Do plants thrive under your thumb? Think about it. We all have talents that we take for granted—abilities that are "no big deal" to us, but are much admired by those who can't do what we can. Those talents have saved us time and money for years. Sharing them with others to brighten their lives is a true gift.

Millions of people of all ages regularly give their talents as volunteers. At last count, the government says about 27 percent of the U.S. population, or 62 million people, volunteer through organizations of all kinds. Many more do so informally. Consider joining a citywide effort to repaint a community center or clean up a school yard. Respond to the next natural disaster instead of standing by and hoping someone else does it. Talk with your family about how to volunteer together. One of the best ways to start is your local United Way. Start at www.liveunited.org.

Give of your treasure

You don't have to consider yourself a "wealthy" person to have riches to share. Think about all those things you and your family own but rarely use—clothing, toys nobody's playing with anymore, and kitchen gadgets you were sure you needed but never touched. Whatever our income or bank account, most of us own more than we need. Hang a shopping bag on the doorknob of every bedroom. Encourage family members to fill them with clothing that's not being worn. If the items are dusty or dirty, make sure they are washed and neatly folded out of respect for the recipient.

Do the same in the kitchen and family room. So many "treasures" can be smartly repurposed, either directly into the hands of those who can wear, use, or play with them, or to nonprofits that are funded by selling used goods. If your child receives three new toys for his birthday, help him pick out three to give away. Encourage a child to use birthday money to purchase a new toy for a child who may have none. The gift of giving is greater than the gift.

In Chapter 10, you'll find some of our best picks for getting involved in the giving movement, including ways to reach out online.

A Bit of You

Kids love nothing more than presenting a gift that they made themselves to a parent or other loved one. Taking the time to help them create one-of-a-kind gifts encourages savings, sure, but it also sends the message that including a bit of yourself in every gift makes it more meaningful.

"A bit of you" can mean so many things. Kids can easily create custom wrapping paper for someone who also loves to give. It's as easy as decorating a roll of white or brown craft paper with words ("A Gift from Gail" or "A Present from Paul") and images that reflect what Gail or Paul is all about. Maybe that bit of you gets baked into a batch of homemade brownies, simply wrapped, and hand-delivered to someone who needs a sweet ending to a not-so-sweet week.

Get inspired by these super-simple ideas for homemade gifts:

Love in a bottle

Making I Love You Jars is a craft that works well with a Scout troop, play group or Sunday school class as a way to honor a deserving someone. Take a recycled, clean glass jar or plastic container. Fill it with slips of paper (picture the inside of a fortune cookie) on which you've written all the reasons why you appreciate Dad, a special teacher, or a friend. Make and decorate a label that fits inside the jar, readable from the outside, with a message like "Thanks for everything, Mom." You might do "Thanks for giving me a love of reading" for a teacher, or "Thanks for sharing your dreams" for a best friend. Help the little ones add stickers, tie a ribbon around the neck of the jar, and add a tag that says who made the jar with love.

Youpons

A "youpon" is like a personalized coupon. It's a promise on paper that says the giver will deliver a special favor, service or creation. A book of youpons makes a perfect holiday or birthday gift from a child to a parent or other relative. These are free and fabulous, and create no waste. Think about what you and your children love to do and do well, and offer youpons to people who appreciate those special abilities. Here are some ideas for youpons you and your kids could make and give:

- An hour of weeding
- A half-day of babysitting
- Cleaning and organizing a closet
- A batch of chocolate-chip cookies
- A home-repair project
- A hug a day for a week
- A picnic in the park with Daddy

- A load of laundry
- Hemming a pair of pants
- A trip to the grocery store
- Six beautifully ironed shirts
- A casserole delivered hot

Another way to do it is to present the youpons with a big batch of "real" coupons, neatly organized by category. We just don't get why anyone would step foot into a grocery store without coupons, but it seems that lots of people are intimidated by the organizing and clipping. The simplest coupon holder in the world is a plastic cardholder box and a set of dividers. Give the gift of savings along with your totally unique youpons.

Picture this

Kids are visual, and many have an amazing eye for photography. Digital photography makes it easy to take endless pictures for "free." A few basic pointers can help a child (or anyone, for that matter) learn to create a really above-average photograph. Even if you don't know much about photography, read up and share a few key points with your kids about lighting, getting close to the subject, and a balanced composition.

There's nothing more personal than a picture, and photos can be made into amazing gifts. If your child photographed a family picnic, birthday party, or graduation, help him or her upload the photos on your computer, select and edit the best ones, and e-mail them, along with a special note, to everyone who was there.

And for grandparents and others who may wish to actually hold and dust a picture frame, choose a print or two and frame them up with a note or poem—a super-satisfying gift that costs next to nothing. (Although you can pay lots for picture frames, you'll find very nice ones at drugstores, often on sale for about $5 for a 4 x 6.)

Also affordable and fun to make and give are digital photo books. Large national retailers, drugstores, and online services let you create photo books of various sizes by uploading your digital photos onto their sites. They're not money-free, but they are money smart. For a very modest amount, you can create a beautiful, personalized photo album. The process is easy enough for kids ages 8 and up. It's creative because they get to design the pages and decide where each photo looks best. What a super gift for a relative serving in the military, or a seldom-seen aunt or uncle.

Paperweights

Because a paperweight lives on a desk, it's a frequent reminder of the person who made and gave it. We like making them because they really come in handy. (We have a thing about cute little crafts that have no purpose . . . but that's a story for another time.) Hunt for some smooth rocks that can be transformed with paint or permanent marker and decorated with odds and ends. We like the idea of keeping a "rock box" for prized rocks. But be sure to watch the signs in parks and conservation areas where it can be illegal to carry out rocks, fossils, etc.

You'll need a nice, smooth stone for the paperweight and some markers or paints to give that gray stone a little pizzazz. Kids can add cool greetings like, "Dad . . . You Rock!" or "Aunt Jane Rocks My World." Be sure the creator adds his or her name and date on the underside. You can also cut out a neat picture from a magazine and attach it to the stone with watered-down glue.

Bag tags

Luggage tags are super handy for spotting yours in a sea of suitcases. Use self-sticking letters to personalize a generic luggage tag. It will always remind the traveler of the special person who thought of this sweet and useful gift.

Stamp of approval

Gently remove stamps from envelopes that come in the mail to create charming gifts. Kids can clip them and keep them in a special place and ask other adults to be on the lookout for cool stamps, as well. Using clear packaging tape, it's easy to collage the used stamps to frames, boxes, used cards, or other surfaces. Cut small pieces of tape and apply over the stamps to create a shiny finish that protects them and holds them in place. This looks very professional! The gift becomes exotic if there are some cool international stamps among the hometown ones.

Just the ticket

This idea works like magic and makes a really unusual gift. Create a decorative bowl (for things, not food or liquid!) from a big roll of tickets left over from a school raffle or bought from the office supply store. Holding the wheel of tickets, gently push out from the center to form a bowl shape. This is so different and ideal for someone who loves plays, movies, and concerts.

These Are So Easy, We Promise

If you keep your antenna up for gifts that you and the kids can make yourselves, you'll come up with all kinds of ideas. It's all about combining what you're good at and like to do—painting, calligraphy, woodworking—with the interests of the person you're gifting.

For those of you with more enthusiasm than hard-core talent (Evie's kind of people), here are some of the easiest and best gifts we know:

Homemade stationery

It takes just a drop of imagination to turn computer paper into personalized stationery right at your computer. Use a variety of fonts, graphics, and images or just big, bold initials to design the stationery. You may like the traditional name and address at the top or bottom, or something more fun like, "A Message from Megan." After the stationery is designed and printed, the sheets can be decorated with stickers. When kids have their own stationery, it encourages them to write letters and thank-you notes. And we all know that a lovely thank-you note is its own gift and an essential social skill.

Now take it to the next level. Take a batch of homemade stationery and make a fun writing kit by adding pens, markers, odds and ends for decorating, and stamps. Put everything in a good-sized zip bag and personalize it with permanent marker. These kits make super birthday party gifts, but they're loved by letter-writers of all ages.

Poet in our midst

Once he gets the hang of it, your child can create wonderful poems and offer them for all kinds of occasions. Robyn recalls the poem she wrote at the age of seven for the bicycle man who fixed her little bike. He framed it and hung it in his shop for decades! Every time Robyn returned to his store, she saw it proudly displayed.

Who knows? It may have inspired her career as an author! (Robyn also became an art teacher, possibly inspired by a first-grade art contest.) There's value and power in helping children nurture their strengths.

Encourage kids to practice rhyming while waiting in line or in the bathtub. The more they do it, the better they'll get. Another way to spark your child's inner poet is by reading the work of old and new poets like Robert Frost, Joyce Kilmer, or Shel Silverstein. Get a stack of poetry books from the library and challenge your child to come up with a few of her own. When it's written or typed on a decorated sheet, rolled, and tied with a piece of ribbon or raffia, a poem is a memorable gift.

Cool pad

Did you know you can create notepads for just a few dollars at a quick copy store? It's perfect for Mother's or Father's Day. The child creates a design, adds the name of the recipient, and maybe a few loving words or a special quote. Take it to the copy shop for "printing and padding." They will scan the design, trim it, and make it into pads with the design on every page. The pads become especially affordable if you have them printed in black and white.

Keep it even simpler by making the pads at home. Help your little one cut recycled computer paper into pad-size pieces, decorate them, then hole-punch and bind the sheets with a brass clip, or secure them with a twisty tie and a yarn bow to create a no-cost pad.

Fancy fringe

One of life's great bargains is close-out fabrics. The stores practically give away yards of great stuff for just pennies. Have fun with fabrics even if you can't sew a stitch. Our friend Anne famously served us cool drinks on a very hot afternoon. She offered darling beverage napkins that we praised. We learned that the fabric, a charming floral pattern, had been her prom dress. Anne's mom was a money-free homemaker who intuitively understood repurposing!

Anne's mom was a great seamstress, but you and your kids can easily make no-sew beverage or appetizer napkins to create a very gift-shop-like gift. Cut fabric into 10" x 10" squares and let the kids fringe the edges to give the fabric an instantly "fancy" finished look. With an age-appropriate tool or a large sewing needle (for older kids), fringe a half-inch edge by simply pulling the threads horizontally to reveal the exposed threads. The edging does not need to be professionally stitched since the fringe will hold up well. Fold each in half twice to create 2.5-inch square napkins.

Tie a pretty ribbon around each set of four or eight and watch the reaction to this great gift. You can also make bread covers or dinner napkins this way. Fringing is an easy way to nicely finish off a square of cloth.

Can-do creations

Everybody needs a pen and pencil holder near the phone or on the desk. Have the kids take a dry can with no sharp edges and decorate it. Then take a stack of same-length pencils, sharpen them up nicely, and add a half dozen inexpensive ballpoint pens. Tie a ribbon around the pens and pencils to hold them in place and give your package a festive touch.

The joy of jars

A scrubbed and dried peanut butter or other type of jar is a blank canvas for all kinds of homemade gifts. Decorate the top, fill the jar with wrapped candies or chocolate kisses, tie a ribbon around the neck, and you're sure to earn a smile. Or have the kids draw a picture on the lid, glue on a special cut-to-fit photograph, or write the recipient's name in fun, collaged letters clipped from a magazine. We use the same idea to make host/hostess gifts by tying a bunch of little candies, homemade cookies, or sugared nuts into a cellophane bag, then securing it with a twisty tie and a little piece of ribbon or raffia.

Four-legged gifting

Kids loving celebrating pets' birthdays. Find plastic or metal water/food bowls on sale at the pet store or big-box retailer. Decorate the outside with permanent marker and paint the name of the pet-cipient. If you've got the time, mix up a batch of wholesome pet treats, fill the bowl with the treats, and wrap the whole thing in cellophane. There are lots of websites with recipes for homemade pet treats. Start with Vetinfo.com and happyhealthy dogs.com.

Lemons into Lemonade

There's a huge category of gifts you can make from existing stuff. We don't mean dust-catching junk. We're talking useful items that can be repurposed, enhanced, or recycled from the hand of someone who doesn't want them or can't use them to someone who can! And that would be you. Check out these possibilities:

Cool tools

Wrap the wooden handle of a recycled or inexpensive hammer with red electrical tape. This takes no time and, so perfect for the holidays, it looks like a candy cane. You can also do this with a broom (no recycling here, these things get dirty!) and gently used garden tools. Make chores more colorful by painting the handles of tools and other objects. Prime them and let the kids paint away, adding special designs all their own. Add a protective finish to make the handle smooth and long-lasting.

Touch of glitz

Transform an everyday object into a shiny treasure. Craft stores have lots of tools for applying rhinestones and other gems. They're not overly expensive, but you could probably find a nice used one on Craigslist. For example, create a great holiday gift for Grandma by starting with an inexpensive pair of reading glasses from the dollar store and adding some fun, faux jewels. The same goes for a cane for an elderly neighbor. Securely glue on-sale trim, twist it tightly around the cane, and secure it at the bottom. Everyone will compliment the cane as Aunt Diana raves about her clever neighbor children who made it for her.

Frame it!

Same idea here. Take a picture frame you have around the house and give it a great new look. Have your daughter dig to the bottom of her toy box and come up with a handful of little toys—a random puzzle piece, tiny animals, dice, or once-loved fast-food meal prizes. Glue them around the perimeter of the frame. (The same technique works for a mirror, too.) When Justin was a little boy, Robyn repurposed a large mirror this way. It hung in his room for years and never failed to attract compliments.

The kids will love seeing their "very own" toys become beautiful decorations for a picture frame or mirror. As with all craft projects, make sure to choose a glue that's safe and appropriate for the surface you're working on. Ask at the craft or hardware store for glue that's non-toxic but very strong since you'll be gluing plastic and other materials to wood.

Quick collages

Posters and other kinds of collages have been popular gifts for ages. Ours are quicker, less messy, and don't require smelly shellac. Start with an object you've got around the house, like poster board, a purse mirror, address book, or blank book. Cut out all the little doodads you want to cover it with—clipped magazine quotes, computer printouts, photos, tickets, photographs, etc. Arrange them attractively, and then "laminate" them into place by covering the entire surface in small pieces of clear packaging tape (the same idea we use for affixing used postage stamps). The tape makes it permanent and glossy—just like shellac but much less messy.

Artful gifts

Turn your child's artwork into bookmarks, mugs, placemats, calendars, and more at any copy shop. These are adorable and make a really affordable way to freeze your child's talent in time with a useful gift somebody will actually use. See what types of things the store can make from artwork you supply by photographing and scanning it. One of the most popular gifts is a customized calendar. We've all seen them, but each one is new and unique because it's your family's treasured photos displayed on the pages. Unlike mugs and key chains, you can make custom calendars on your own computer by uploading photos of your kids' artwork. Search online for "printable calendars." There are lots of options, most of them free.

Wrapping and Decorating

Creating a great-looking gift can really get expensive. That's one of the reasons we love to recycle gift wrap. There are lots of other ways to personalize your package using things you've got around or have repurposed from other projects. Start with gift wrap. Who said wrapping paper has to be used only once, printed on both sides, heavy, and cost an arm and a leg? We love to use fun and funky papers like the Sunday comics and old maps that cost next to nothing, but make gifts stand out. Add stickers, labels, and one-of-a-kind gift toppers to kick it up.

To recycle actual wrapping paper, roll it on a cardboard tube to eliminate as many creases as you can. Combine bits and bigger pieces of papers that don't necessarily "match." Strategic folding and two-sided taping can help you create a smoothly wrapped package that's charming, eclectic, or funky. Kids can add stickers, drawings, and images printed from the Internet, cut out from comic books, the phone book, or magazines.

Make Robyn's funky and fun Trash Bag Roses for a more dramatic package. Check out her book *Make It Memorable* for creative DIY ideas. They're really impressive and easy to make from a new thirteen-gallon white plastic trash bag. Cut strips that are twenty-four inches long and two inches wide from the trash bag. Using a needle and thread, "stitch" the side of the strip under and over until pulling on it makes it begin to spiral into a rose shape. A beautiful flower will start to emerge before your eyes. Finish off the rose with a knot to hold the stitches and attach it with pipe cleaners or twisty ties. You'll need to closely supervise children, as this craft requires a needle, scissors, and a plastic bag.

Another way to perk up your package is to take gently used wrapping paper, fold it (accordion-style) into a pretty fan, and add it to the top of a gift. This lends a rich department-store look to a homemade gift. Add an accompanying note that announces, "With love from your biggest fan!"

Another sweet add-on is the Tootsie Pop Bouquet. Carefully insert a bunch of Tootsie Pops into a piece of Styrofoam to cover the surface, or simply gather them up with recycled ribbons and tie the bouquet onto the package. These also make wonderful centerpieces for birthday parties.

Stuck on someone? Chances are that you've got a box of blank, sticky-back labels somewhere in a closet or office drawer. Let the kids use these to design a collection of stickers that's all about who they are and what they love. These can be cut out of the label or, even easier, let the designs fill the shape and size of the label. Use stickers that include your child's name to seal homemade greeting cards.

How about a gift of personalized return address labels or gift-card stickers? It's easy to create these on the computer from printer-friendly labels. Work with the kids to create their own gift-card labels that say "A Gift from Jenna" or "Love from Leah." A few pages of these, rolled and tied, make a great gift. And when you attach one to a birthday party gift, it's much more likely to be seen than an easy-to-lose card. Keep a bunch of these on hand. You'll save money on greeting cards, and the sticker will identify the giver.

Sharpen your pencil because in Chapter 8 we share ideas for cutting the cost of all things school, from what your kids wear to what they eat from September to June. The ideas get an A-plus for saving money and keeping the school day relaxed for everyone in the family.

8

Super School Savings

WHEN WE THINK ABOUT THE COST of raising children, expenses associated with going to school might not be the first thing that comes to mind. But, in fact, learning can be pricey, even if your kids are enrolled in public school. When we really started to focus on school, from getting dressed to getting supplies to getting good grades, we realized that the school day is packed with opportunities to provide our kids with opportunities to learn and grow in a comfortable environment without overspending.

This chapter gets high marks for its blend of common sense and innovation. We love and use ideas like a money-saving supply closet that we stock with close-out and clearance finds. (It's also a great way to put the kids in charge of their own project deadlines. No more, "Mom, we have to go to the store *right now* for a project that's due tomorrow!") We've got ideas for jazzing up school lunches, making tutoring and homework help more accessible and affordable, and creatively filling those after-school hours.

You can't control what goes on inside the classroom, but you can do a lot to make those nine all-important months more enjoyable for your family.

Write the Rules, Set the Tone

School days are packed for even the youngest students. Depending on your children's transportation and after-school schedule, they can be out of the house for more than ten hours a day. Getting up and out five days in a row is no small feat. How do you keep up the schedule and reduce the stress?

Rules are tools to help you do this. In the same way that you always keep the peanut butter on the middle shelf of the pantry and require beds to be made every morning (you do, don't you?!), you need school-day rules. At first blush, you might think this sounds demanding and stress-inducing, but, in fact, the opposite is true. When children know the expectations, there's less negotiating and whining, and, ultimately, more cheerful compliance.

Every family has to establish the rules that work for them. Once you've drafted them, review them with your children, make any changes, type them up, print them, and stick them in a plastic sleeve. Give every member of the family a copy and keep one in the kitchen.

Here are a few sample rules that can help everyone move through the school day more smoothly and without too much last-minute rushing around. The rules you ultimately use will depend on things like the age of your children and your work schedule.

- **WAKE-UP PLAN.** We think by around age eight (and possibly younger) kids should be able to set and wake up to an alarm clock. There's no reason for a high-school student to rely on Mom or Dad to get her out of bed. Soon, this young woman will be in college. Who's going to gently tap on her door to wake her then? The plan should center on a set wake-up time and before-school expectations, like making the bed and straightening the room.
- **SCHOOL-DAY TASKS.** Moms like to think they've got the corner on it, but multitasking is a skill that kids of all ages can learn. During the school year, multitasking means chores in addition to school work. These jobs should be identified on your rule sheet. They aren't "favors" to Mom, and they don't require dramatic praise or rewards. It's an expectation that helps everyone. Kyle fills and empties the dishwasher. Sara brings in the mail and waters the plants on Friday. The tasks are done without complaint from the child and without nagging from the parents. Consequences for not doing them are established and spelled out in your rules.
- **MENU PLAN.** The important thing about lunch is that it be healthy, eaten, and enjoyed. So insisting that your kids eat at school or bring from home is counter-productive if the food gets tossed and your poor kid has a growling stomach during PE. We think school-age kids can decide for themselves if they buy or bring, provided there is a choice and your budget allows it. Some parents find bringing lunch actually costs them more, while other resourceful moms find they save a bundle. But they need to let you know in advance what they plan to do. That way you can avoid last-minute runs for lunch fixings. Review the online menu with your child over the weekend, decide on a game plan, and stick to it.

- **AFTER-SCHOOL ROUTINE.** Remember how good it felt to get home from school, grab a snack, and run outside to play? Kids need to decompress after a day in the classroom, whether it's by riding bikes, listening to music, having a friend over, or watching a limited amount of approved TV. Without over-programming, your rules should describe the after-school priorities. So on days with no after-school activities, the kids are free to play with neighbor kids, relax with a book or video game, etc. Spelling it out doesn't mean everything will go like clockwork; it just means there is a vision.

- **THE BASICS.** This is where you spell out the basics like hanging up jackets, and stowing boots and book bags. Younger kids especially need a designated space to store their belongings. The rules spell out how to reach Mom and Dad, contact information for the neighbors, and what to do in an emergency when babysitters are present or when children enter the home without an adult present. A quick text to let Mom know that a teen has arrived safely at home or another after-school destination is a common expectation.

Performance and response. Getting paid for A's just never made that much sense to us, but many families believe it's a reasonable way to acknowledge school success. Although it's controversial, school districts in many parts of the country are rewarding kids with cash, concert tickets, and other goodies. There are lots of reasons this may not be a good idea. For example, for kids with learning challenges, the A's may never materialize despite lots of effort. How you acknowledge good school work and effort is up to you. Maybe it's a "favorite dinner" each marking period for good grades, or a week-long break from chores if a school conference reveals that a child has been trying his best.

Establishing rules is really establishing an approach. It's not about hard and fast mandates as much as a vision that helps keep everybody on an even keel (at least most of the time).

Getting Organized

We're both big believers in order, not just because it makes your house look and run better, but because you spend less, waste less, and have more time for your family when you know what you've got and you're not living in a mess. You don't have to be a neat freak or expect your kids to tow the line perfectly, but there will be plenty of payback if you buy into some basic principles.

Supplies and demand

Nothing beats that "brand-new-nothing-torn-or-broken" feeling of back-to-school supplies. The clean book bag, big pack of markers, and un-dogeared binders create excitement like little else. Whether your child is heading to pre-school with crayons or tackling calculus with a graphing calculator, she needs an amazing amount of stuff to succeed.

But here's an urgent memo—the time to do back-to-school shopping isn't the couple weeks before school. Sure, you'll find helpful specials and promotions then, including tax-free holidays in some states. But if you create a year-round plan, you won't have the rush-out-to-buy syndrome. The smarter bet is to create a supply closet (or a couple of drawers in an old dresser or some decent plastic bins) stocked with things you buy on closeout and clearance whenever you find them. Be constantly on the lookout for steals on markers, cardboard, foam core, glue sticks, fabric scraps, safety scissors, pencils, notebooks, binders, etc.

You're still going to need to fulfill the back-to-school list sent by the school or teacher. But for those endless at-home projects and other needs throughout the year, you'll save a ton and always have things on hand if you buy cheap and in advance.

A word about textbooks: Although most public schools provide students with books, that's not the case at parochial and private schools. It's also true that when books are provided, some are in short supply due to budget cutbacks. Some parents like to have a second copy of each book to keep at home. You can cut the cost dramatically by swapping with other families and/or buying used or discounted books, especially online. Follett Educational Services (fes.follett.com), Amazon.com, and half.com (an eBay site) are good starting points. As with any discount purchase, know your prices before assuming you're getting a good deal. Craigslist can be helpful, when used with caution. Another tactic is to type the name and edition of the book for which you're searching on Google or another search engine along with the word "used."

Storing and transporting school stuff

When you help your kids get and stay organized with school-work, you're teaching lessons for a lifetime. You're also giving them a leg up on school success—no more zeroes for missing papers stuck randomly in a book that should have been placed in the math binder!

Donna Goldberg, author of the award-winning book *The Organized Student* (organizedstudent.com), says you need to help your kids create a system of organization within their backpacks that allows them to take the necessary materials to and from school. Use a binder or accordion file specifically from storing loose paper and materials that are not currently necessary for class.

Students should go through their school desks periodically in the same way, whether or not the teach required it. If your child is old enough to have a locker, consider getting a locker shelf, an inexpensive purchase that allows kids to easily organize their space.

Managing minutes

Help your children learn one of the most valuable lessons school can teach—managing time. From about third grade on, kids can efficiently use a calendar. You can buy one, but there are lots of options for downloading them for free. Check out keepandshare. com, calendar.google.com, or cozi.com, which offers a free family organizer. Neat stuff.

Fight germs

A little bit of organization can also help keep germs and viruses away from your home and family. That means fewer trips to the doctor or clinic, and fewer lost days of work and income for you. Try this simple idea: Ask everyone who lives in your home to wash with soap and water every time they enter the house. Stock the bathroom with pump soap and paper towels, and be sure the sink can be reached safely by the shortest members of your household. And while you're at it, ask other children who visit to wash up upon arriving as well.

Purchase a small container of hand sanitizer for your child's book bag, desk, and/or locker. Save by buying the large size and refilling the smaller ones. Explain to the kids why hand washing is so important and the fact that we all need to take responsibility for our own health and the health of others. And, of course, you'll want to mirror the behaviors you're asking of them. Family culture plays a huge role in our future habits.

Get More Out of Your Home

A house that works well is more fun and easier to live in any time of year. But we find that when school is in session and everyone's super busy, living orderly really helps keep down the crazies. Among our favorite home management ideas:

- **SHOP SMARTER.** Ask every member of the family who can to list supplies that you've run out of like toothpaste, notebook paper, favorite snacks, etc., on a whiteboard posted in the kitchen. In this way, the parent who shops knows exactly what's needed and can buy ahead in money-saving quantities. It's the last-minute purchases that can really bust the budget and cost you time.

- **MAKE RECYCLING EASY.** It doesn't take much effort to place cardboard, newspaper, and plastic in separate bins in the garage. Recycling is good for the planet, especially if Mom and Dad are getting some help.

- **GO THROUGH CLOSETS REGULARLY.** Collect clothing and other items to be given away or sold at a garage sale. Help kids learn to assess what's too small or what's not getting played with anymore. Doing this regularly also helps keep closets from getting filled with things nobody's wearing. Then you know what you've got and can avoid buying what you don't need.

- **A PLACE FOR EVERYTHING.** And we mean everything. Sports equipment goes in the wheelbarrow in the garage, not all over the yard after it's played with. Putting away balls, bats, and jump ropes keeps them in better shape and less likely to need replacement. Towels go on hooks or refolded on towel bars, not on the floor or the hamper. Doing unnecessary laundry is expensive and environmentally costly.

• **HOME SWEET MINE.** Kids will take better care of their home if they're invested in it. Create this investment by working on a home fix-it project as a family. Instead of hiring a contractor, do some research and install that new mini-brick fireplace yourselves. Build some raised beds to expand your backyard garden. You can have a really fun, productive weekend that doesn't involve the mall, and the result is a home improvement everybody will love. Take a break from the work/homework routine to improve your home . . . together.

Eliminating Homework Headaches

There's a huge controversy raging out there about homework—when, how much, the role of parents, etc. We'll leave this one to parents and professional educators to sort out, but suffice it to say that homework is here to stay. Our job is to help you keep it from overwhelming your kids and your budget. You will notice an editorial slant that we really can't help—the view that homework should be a way for children to learn, not a way for parents to learn. Like us, you've already done the school thing. Now it's their turn.

Sharon Marshall Lockett, Director of Lockett Learning Systems/Score at Score-ed.com, agrees that it's super important to give a child the freedom and independence to do the assigned work as best he or she can. That doesn't mean parents shouldn't answer questions or help prepare for a test. But what starts with innocent "help" on a pre-school project ends up with parents completing college applications for their kids and, we're not kidding, calling up potential employers to ask why their "child" didn't get picked for a job. Plant the seeds of self-reliance early.

Okay, we're off the soapbox now and onto some really good tips for happier homework.

Homework central

Every student needs a designated homework spot. It might be the kitchen for the little ones and a bedroom desk for the older kids. In some families, everybody gathers around the dining-room table for a kind of study hall. The older kids help the younger ones. Sometimes, everybody benefits from a change of scenery. Suggest an occasional outdoor homework session, or drop off teens at the library or coffee shop. They'll think it's cool and so will you, especially if they come back with the history paper written.

Think creatively

Homework projects like science experiments can get expensive, especially if the whole thing has to be done several times. Look for parts and supplies at stores that are going out of business. Think about your workplace. Lots of things get tossed that can be creatively repurposed into school projects.

Save money on tutors

If your kids attend day care or an after-school program, you should expect that homework help and tutoring are part of what you're paying for. Many school districts have homework help lines and services. Community centers and places of worship offer this type of help, too. At some community colleges, students involved in teaching-related workshops tutor as part of their own studies. You can also "trade kids" for tutoring help with a neighbor or family members. Sometimes, the lesson is more readily learned when it comes from someone who isn't Mom or Dad. And don't forget to get the grandparents involved. They love sharing knowledge and experience.

Check out online homework resources

Get recommendations from other parents who have used these, read online reviews, and spend some time on a site before letting your child use it. Make sure the service really is free and be vigilant to the possibility of someone trying to inappropriately gain access to your child. A valuable website filled with guidance on this topic is math-and-reading-help-for-kids.org, which is associated with the American Library Association.

You'll find articles about online homework help, the parent's role in education, homeschooling, parenting tips, helping children with disabilities, and child development, as well as math problems and worksheets.

The site also lists questions that parents searching for online educational assistance should ask of the help sites they review.

1. Who created the website?
2. When was the site last updated?
3. Is it easy to find the needed information?
4. Does the information seem to be correct when you compare it to class notes, textbooks, or other websites?

Reward with activities rather than gifts

If the homework is done early and well, how about a thirty-minute backyard catch or a game of HORSE out on the basketball court? If you have two or more children, reward them with some one-on-one time doing something they love to do, such as a bike ride or a walk to the ice-cream shop just with you. Some parents think doing what you should is its own reward, but that's your call! We think a little pat on the back can help motivate kids.

Think inside the box

If your children do homework at a table or at a desk shared with other members of the family, create a Happy Homework Box for each student. It contains everything needed for a successful homework session, from pencils and erasers to loose notebook paper, and maybe a little bag of homemade granola for energy. This can cut down the time-wasting associated with getting started. It's also fun. Younger students will enjoy decorating and personalizing the box. A plastic shoe box (typically about $2) makes a good container.

Don't be pound foolish

Sometimes in our efforts to help our children and save money, we can be penny wise and pound foolish. Homework issues are an example. If you have constant squabbles about homework that repeat themselves day after day, you may need outside help. An hour or two of professional counseling might reveal some patterns you could never have seen yourself, but that are causing daily friction between you and your child and affecting others in the family. Every community has social workers or psychologists who specialize in these kinds of issues. If you decide to see someone, ask your school counselor. He or she will likely have resources to get you started. Working with the school can also lead to a team approach that will ultimately help your child.

Look Great for Less

Nothing felt quite as good as putting on that special dress or shirt that you absolutely loved wearing to school. Remember how confident you felt when you laced up your favorite sneakers or slipped into those super-cool boots? Those feelings are timeless and universal, and your child has them, too. The only problem is the price tag. With some designer jeans and sneakers in the triple-digit range, looking good in class can be an expensive proposition.

At many private schools and a growing number of public school districts, requiring school uniforms has been one approach to solving the problem. But most parents still face the challenge of finding and funding affordable, appropriate school clothes. (One smart mom whose kids were required to wear uniforms exchanged hand-me-downs with a family with kids of different sizes. They were able to save quite a bit on uniforms, especially on those occasional pieces that were required but seldom worn.)

If you're reading this book, you're probably a pretty savvy shopper, but check out our tips for cutting the cost of school couture.

Shop consignment stores

Every town and city in America (well, most) has excellent consignment stores where you can buy gently used children's clothing. If your child is a 'tween or older, shopping for used clothing can even be cool. Have the kids try on things in the store and look over your purchases carefully. You probably won't be able to return things as you can in retail stores. If you've got a problem with used clothing, get over it. Wash everything you bring home and share the kids' excitement at having awesome "new" clothes that didn't cost you a fortune.

The electronic version of consignment stores is eBay and other sites where used merchandise is sold. You don't have to be an expert to find a good deal on eBay, but you do have to be smart and aware. Talk to people who have experience buying on these sites and learn about the pitfalls. The site has its own learning pages for buyers and sellers (pages.ebay.com/education), and the Internet is filled with tips and opinions.

Use coupons strategically

These days, coupons are just the beginning when it comes to discounts. Multiply their value by using them in combination with special offers ("Midnight Madness," "Labor Day blowout," "20% off all day Saturday") to exponentially enhance their value.

Avoid impulse buying

Develop a list and try to avoid clothes shopping on the fly. Plan your outings during sales tax holidays, clearance sales, and other money-saving times. Many experts say full-price retail is a thing of the past. Even the finest stores have sales, and if you wait, you can probably get that gorgeous whatever for a lot less than when you or your daughter first fell in love with it.

Click before you go

Before you head out, check the website of the stores you're heading to for any unadvertised online specials that may not have been in the paper. These are more common at large, national stores, but smaller retailers are getting into the act as well.

Get comfortable with online shopping

Shopping via the Internet is here to stay. The beauty of it is the convenience, but it takes some discipline to get past those full-price items on the home page and snake around to the sales. Avoid the temptation to put anything in your "shopping cart" that you don't intend to buy. The same rules apply to shopping in stores—come in with a budget, a list, and willpower. Unless it's on a fabulous sale and you or your child absolutely needs it, leave it behind. A week later, you'll never remember those pricey jeans or the boots that seemed irresistible.

Patience pays in the virtual shopping world, too. We personally only shop sites with free shipping and returns. But if you're on a site that charges to send and/or return, take the time to call the toll-free number (or click for live chat) and ask if you can get free shipping via any special promotions or simply because it's Tuesday! Retailers want your business and, these days, they're going farther than ever to get and keep it.

Squirrel it away

If you find yourself strapped for cash at the beginning of each school year, consider a simple monthly savings plan to get you where you want to be by August. Figure out how much you'll want to spend and divide it into twelve. Put away that amount each month in its own bank or online savings account. Then when it's time to outfit the kids, you'll have what you need and a built-in budget to boot.

The Lunch Bill Ringeth

We don't know about you, but there was always something about sitting in class that made us ravenously hungry! A good lunch is a much-anticipated part of the school day. Most school lunch programs are highly subsidized and, as such, quite affordable. Some are even making progress in offering healthier choices. But if you or your child doesn't like what's served, you're throwing out money—and food—every day. Worse yet, your child is trying to learn on an empty stomach, definitely a losing proposition.

Preparing a nutritious and affordable lunch for the kids is easy. Packing something they'll actually like and eat is a little bit tougher. Our idea starters can keep things interesting for the kids, and efficient for Mom and Dad.

- **MAKE LUNCHES WHILE YOU'RE PUTTING AWAY DINNER.** There's a lot to be said for a yummy lunch that includes a hearty chef salad based on last night's chicken vs. a sandwich made with fatty lunch meat and mayonnaise. It may take a few more minutes to assemble, but the results can be delicious and healthful. Even if lunch is not based on last night's meal, get the lunches packed while you're in the kitchen.
- **STUDY WHAT YOU'RE SPENDING.** School lunches are just a part of your weekly food budget, but it all adds up. Periodically (maybe once every few months), review several weeks' grocery store receipts and take inventory of what you're buying and what you're using. It's easy to get into a food-buying rut. If you find yourself with three packages of uneaten cinnamon-raisin English muffins, you can be pretty sure they don't belong on next week's list. Everybody's tastes and preferences change, and

you've got to keep your buying in tune with what your family is eating now, not what they ate six months ago.

- **ELIMINATE THE "HIDDEN" COSTS.** It may not be the family pack of chicken and bulk toilet paper that are doing you in. But you're probably spending more than needed on snacks, beverages, and other "small" items. Foods like quality energy bars and whole-grain snacks—the stuff you want your kids to eat—can get quite expensive when you consider the per-serving price. Instead, mix up a batch of homemade oatmeal cookies (a good basic recipe is usually on the canister of oats) and purchase a sturdy beverage bottle so you can buy large quantities of juice rather than sending individually packaged drinks.

- **DON'T SHOP WITHOUT 'EM.** Coupons can put a serious dent in your weekly food budget. You don't have to be one of those people who spends three hours a day clipping and cataloging. We estimate fifteen minutes a week can easily save you $15.

Don't Make After School an Afterthought

The most costly, potentially chaotic part of a school day can be after the bell rings. That's when art lessons, scouts, math tutoring, gymnastics, soccer, keyboard lessons, and hip hop dance class get under way. Eeek! Enriching our kids' lives should be the goal of after-school activities, not driving them or you crazy with too much stimuli and impossible schedules.

Before the school year begins, sit down with your children and discuss what activities they would like to participate in and why. Now give *your* opinions. Your daughter may want to join a choir that meets three times a week in another town because her best friend Beth is in it. It's your job to explain that Beth loves to sing, while reminding your daughter that she can't carry a tune and is really much more interested in sports. It's not hard to get caught up in that sticky activity web, wanting your children to join something just because someone else's child is doing it. Be strong, and if it doesn't make sense, just say no!

Exposing children to the arts, sports, religious education, and other kinds of enrichment isn't a contest. In fact, many experts say the winners are the kids who are allowed to do less and play more—the ones who aren't caught up in rushing from activity to activity, filling up on fast food, and changing from softball uniform to skating skirt in the car.

Ask these questions as you consider after-school activities:

- Has your child shown interest in the activity beyond the fact that a friend is doing it?
- Is it convenient in terms of location and schedule?
- Is the price in keeping with your budget?
- What are the conditions and consequences? (If your child decides to quit, how much have you lost? If he can't make it for this week's lesson, can you apply the payment to another lesson or have you lost your money?)
- Is the individual or entity offering the enrichment reputable? Have you talked with other parents who have used this vendor and/or checked Internet reviews?
- How much total time is required, and is this acceptable?
- Will the activity be stressful or overwhelming to your child? (You're right. It is hard to anticipate this in advance, but your parental intuition is probably correct.)
- Does the activity leave time for unstructured play and exploration?

Lessons and the like can really get expensive, but there are ways you can trim the cost. We recommend establishing an activities budget for each child. Like all allocations of this type, don't expect the exact same expenditure for Max, who loves free community T-ball, as for Caroline, who's a promising pianist taking private lessons. Get a pretty good idea of what you're going to spend and stick to your guns.

There are some ways around that potentially expensive rate you're seeing. Some studios and organizations ask for the entire payment up front, which lets them use your money for months at a time. This may be negotiable, but you'll never know if you don't ask. If you do pay in advance, this should be accompanied by a percentage discount. And if you pay on a credit card, check your statement each month to be sure that only the monthly fee has been charged.

Other ways to cut costs include asking about any scholarship funds that may be available but not well-publicized. Also, see if you can barter your services for your child's participation. For example, you might be able to coach a Little League team, help with cleanup in the pottery studio, or be responsible for all e-mail correspondence for a twirling team your daughter is dying to join. (If you barter for professional services, there may be a tax implication, so be sure to run this by your tax preparer if you have one.) Also, don't hesitate to ask your child to be part of the solution. For example, your ten-year-old can help with laundry, giving you more time for a home-based freelance job, which permits her to visit that riding stable every week!

If the whole after-school runaround turns you off, you might like to create your own extracurricular programming or do it with friends or neighbors. Think about it as home school for activities. The key to making this work is committing to it, as you would to an activity you paid for. Here are a few ideas:

- **CRAFTY WEDNESDAYS.** Have a surprise craft project waiting for your kids once a week. Make it seasonal, tie it to a family birthday, or base it on some fun materials you find around the house.
- **CHECKERS AND CHESS CLUB.** Teach your kids to play these timeless classics and see how long it takes for them to start beating you. Like an after-school or community club, make it a six- or ten-week commitment, and offer a little prize for the winner.
- **EXCHANGE AND ENGAGE.** Create classes within your neighborhood. You do a three-week session on jewelry-making, and a neighbor hosts the kids for three weeks of pottery. This way, kids get to experience lots of enrichment, and the choices are probably more exciting than your standard after-school offerings.
- **BOOT CAMP.** Work with your child to create a fitness program you can do together a couple of afternoons a week. Maybe one day is tennis, and the second day is bike riding. Put it on the calendar and really make it happen.
- **OUR TOWN.** Discover some of those great gems that visitors to your community enjoy but you never find time for, like a small history museum, a cool trail, local beach, etc. Take an after-school field trip to one site a week for six or eight weeks. Decide what places you'd like to return to with the whole family for a longer outing.
- **DINNER CLUB.** Get your kids involved in menu planning and cooking that night's meal. It's a wonderful way to learn about nutrition, shopping, and using in-season produce. If you can grab your recycled shopping bags and walk to the grocery store for ingredients you might need, even better.
- **MY CLUB.** You may never find a club that focuses on old trains or learning Portuguese, but it's no problem if you create the

club yourself. Help your child research what he or she is interested in, then find and pursue local resources.

- **FREE COMMUNITY OFFERINGS.** Hold onto your wallet. If your community is like most, it offers tons of kids' enrichment activities for free or for a very nominal cost. Check with your town or city hall, city parks/recreation department, or department of children's services.

Private vs. Public

Getting a preschooler into the most popular (and likely expensive) private school can take on huge importance for parents in some communities. Before you make that decision and commitment, thoroughly investigate your options. Some parents we talked with agree that what initially seemed like an absolute must was ultimately not the right choice. While private schools can offer an outstanding education, these parents found what they were looking for and could afford at quality public or charter schools, especially when they were able to get involved in the school. We reserve judgment, but have found that our children have been well-served at public schools as well as in private schools that best served their needs and learning styles. The challenge is to find a match, then pursue all available resources to determine what can work best for your child and family.

Your kids live in a highly wired world. How do you get them involved but not let the gadgets take over? We cover that and more in Chapter 9.

From Wii to We—
Techno Kids, 'Tweens,
and Teens

KIDS AND PARENTS love technology. Electronic gadgets have become an inescapable and beneficial part of our lives. But cell phones, handheld computers, laptops, and video games can put a serious dent in the family budget. The question "Mommy, can I have a cell phone?" is coming earlier and earlier. But the digital world can be isolating and keep us from connecting with others. We love technology as much as anybody, but we're looking for that balance we think is achieved when there's "more we and less Wii" around the house.

This chapter offers age-appropriate ideas to help everyone enjoy technology appropriately and affordably. We're thinking outside the electronic box, with alternatives to the marketing messages that entice kids to demand the latest gizmos, like our Family Concert Series right in your own home and our must-see section on helping your child get really good at technology while keeping your computers in working order! Parents will love the fresh thinking and big savings. Kids will love the cool new ways to plug in.

Best Seat in the House

Ever since we were young (back when there were only three channels and one movie on Saturday night!), cuddling up on the couch to watch a flick has always been a favorite activity. It's still one of the most affordable ways to spend quality family time. Of course, now there are video rental stores, Netflix, TNT, On Demand and many other options. But even if you have the most basic cable or satellite package, you've still got loads of choices. You don't even need cable—public TV alone offers many wonderful movies.

But did you ever think of kicking your family viewing experience up a notch? You can explore the "culture universe" for pennies per performance when you do it on DVD. Why not create a Family Concert Series? Depending on how many people are in your family and how many weeks you want the series to last, everyone gets one or more choices of what will be seen.

We can read your mind. You're thinking that your ten-year-old wants to see the Jonas Brothers, you'd love see a performance by The Boston Pops, and your husband is all about Martina McBride. But here's the deal—everybody is encouraged to enjoy one another's picks. No criticism, no put-downs of other people's favorites. Just a couple hours of entertainment and the chance to expand everyone's musical horizons without footing the bill for four or five concerts.

Like any good concert series, you'll want to make sure yours is well-promoted. Assign talented family members the jobs of designing a logo, making tickets, and writing up a flyer that includes the required who, what, where, and when. Pick someone else to be in charge of the refreshment stand, an important part of any entertainment outing. Change it up each week—maybe popcorn balls one week and ice-cream sundaes the next.

The kids will love creating their own special event. Turn them *loose within limits* (we love this term—it really says so much about how we think) and watch what they come up with. You may even want to have some fun by requiring that everyone wear clothes to match the era or the performance. Dress up in hippie garb for a Beatles or Simon and Garfunkel concert. If Mom chooses an opera, it's a great excuse for the kids to get fancy, maybe even borrowing an old gown or tux from Mom and Dad's closet.

No concert is complete until the reviews are in. If one of your children likes to write, ask him to write a review of the concert. Encourage him to get quotes from those who attended and explain why the artist delighted or disappointed the fans. Post it on the refrigerator for all to see why a particular performer got three, four or no stars!

This activity can be a blast for the family, but there's a solid learning component, for sure. Being able to cheerfully accept someone else's preferences is one of life's most important lessons. We'll roll out the red carpet for that kind of thinking any day.

Click Fresh, Click Free

It's easy to fall into an Internet rut. We find ourselves going to the same sites all the time, forgetting that there's a world of new things to see and learn online. Time-strapped parents may regularly visit the websites of their kids' schools and do some online sale shopping, but not much more. Kids get into patterns, too.

Depending on what parents allow, they may play their favorite online games, visit approved websites, or IM or Facebook their friends.

We've searched the Internet for sites that let you jazz up your online experience without opening your wallet. Pull up an extra chair or two to the computer, sit down with a child or two, and sample a few of these. Get input from the kids, but you be the decider-in-chief about what online activities are okay for your family.

- **KIDSITES.COM.** A good overview of the online family universe. Plan to spend some time clicking through before deciding what the kids should visit; it's an investment in time you won't regret.
- **KABOOSE.COM.** Lots of solid content on crafts, activities, health, food, and more.
- **GIRLSENSE.COM.** Financial information and neat activities for your female 'tween.
- **CLUBPENGUIN.COM.** From Disney, a safe game site with a good parent guide.
- **GLUBBLE.COM.** Provides the safety of downloading an entire browser, plus cool activities like a family photo timeline.
- **BLOGSAFETY.COM** or **CONNECTSAFELY.ORG.** Good sites to learn about blogging. Learn about the benefits and pitfalls before you decide if starting a blog could work for your child. We also love the idea of a jointly written child/parent blog. There are so many possibilities out there—write about family life from two perspectives, blog about shared interests like sports or pets, or find an unfilled niche.
- **CALENDAR.GOOGLE.COM.** People love using Google calendar to get the family's schedules in sync and organized. It's easy to set up each person with his or her own calendar, then share all the information. You can be on it in no time.

Beyond the Click

There's so much you can do for free on the Internet to expand your world and connect to others.

- **VIDEO CHAT.** Want to make sure your kids "see" out-of-town grandparents or other relatives more often? Try video chatting with Gmail video chat (Mail.google.com/videochat), which is free if you have Gmail. Another option, Skype (Skype.com), will cost you about three dollars per month. To video chat on Skype, you'll need a computer with a built-in video camera. (Most of the new ones have them.) In addition to the video feature, the services also let you make "free" long-distance calls when you're out of town or out of the country. If your parents are out of town, Skype can be a super way for them to connect with the children. Our friends, Lynn and Wink, Skype regularly with grandson Eli across the country. They sing, play music, put on puppet shows, and generally have a blast making this essential connection. Well before his first birthday, Eli would squeal and giggle when they appeared on the screen.
- **MAKE AND SEND ONLINE CARDS.** Have you noticed how expensive greeting cards have gotten? We want our children to remember special occasions, but at three dollars or more per card, being gracious is costly. There are many good sites for making cards for free. We like to check out BlueMountain. com and MyCardmaker.com.
- **DISCOVER D.C.** The federal government operates lots of great websites for kids. Kids.gov is the portal to all of them, and there's always something new to see. We had a great time checking out some of the instructive and fun websites. NASA has a

variety of sites that can be seen and accessed through NASA.gov. If you and your children love space exploration, you'll want to spend some time together at spaceplace. NASA.gov. Also check out games.noaa.gov for interactive fun based on the ocean and air. The site is operated by the National Ocean and Atmospheric Administration. Kids.clerk.house.gov takes you to Kids in the House, a very cool way to learn about Congress, take a virtual field trip to the U.S. Capitol, and learn how a bill becomes law. Smallstep.gov/kids is the site of Small Step Kids, all about food, what it can do for you, and why it matters so much.

- LEARN ABOUT FAMOUS PEOPLE. Travel back in time with your child and learn about amazing people like Helen Keller at the Helen Keller Kids Museum Online. The easiest way to get there is through AFB.org, the American Federation for the Blind site. From there, click on "Information for Kids." There's great content, including games about Braille and the world of the blind. The online museum is wonderful, too.
- HAVE A DIGITAL DIP. A rich (pun intended) site, benandjerrys. com, is operated by the Vermont ice-cream people. There are games and seasonal crafts, plus information about protecting the environment and the activism category Ben and Jerry call "Peace, Love, and Ice Cream."

Reading Readiness

The Internet is filled with sites to help kids learn to read. Whether you want your pre-schooler clicking away on websites at a tender age is your call. What we can say is that there are lots of safe, content-rich websites. Always, do your own checking and make sure a site matches your preferences and individual goals. We're not educational experts, but we like a few of these especially and believe in cautiously exposing young children to the Internet— always with supervision, of course.

- **READINGROCKETS.ORG** (you might recognize the name from the PBS kids' show) is an easy-to-navigate site with information for parents and educators about helpful reading strategies, struggling readers, learning disabilities, and educational technologies.
- **STARFALL.COM** is a popular site that offers affordable educational products, materials, stories, games, and songs that encourage early reading.
- **BESTHOMESCHOOLING.ORG** has lots of content for homeschooling parents that's also valuable for any parent. There are lessons, articles, excerpts from relevant books, personal stories, and best practices.
- **MOMSHOMEROOM.MSN.COM** is a neat site with articles, a message board, tips from teachers, and articles about school success.

Techno Time-Out

For kids who have never known a world without portable DVD players and electronic books, it's hard to imagine life without modern technology. We think perspective is a good thing, especially if it helps kids appreciate their lives. And one of the best ways to get perspective is to take a techno time-out for one or more days, even a week if you dare.

That's right, we're talking about turning off the electronics— powered down, really off. It may seem like a charming or instructive exercise (we think it's both), but think hard before you leap. It's not as easy as you think, and it definitely takes some planning. The goal is to help children understand that communication is not the telephone and art is not the DVD player. These are just the devices we've developed to help us do and enjoy things. Homework, frustration, disagreements with friends, parents, and homework pressures are the real stuff in life. We just experience all of it through the filter of technology.

If you do try unplugging for a while (and we hope you will), decide on the rules ahead of time, based on your family's priorities. You may wish to include the children in establishing the rules. Doing so makes it more likely that they'll participate fully. You'll want to write out a plan and a goal, and ask everyone in pre-school and older to sign it to show their commitment.

For example, "Our family's techno time-out will start April 4 at noon and end April 5 at 7 p.m. During that time, we will not use computers, televisions, CD and DVD players, video games, or personal digital assistance devices. Our goal is to understand what life is like when we rely more on ourselves than on electronics."

You'll need to make other decisions, too, like whether you will use your phone and, if so, will it be for emergencies only? Some families even go cold turkey on the car, which can really change your life. Of course, you need a weekend of few plans with anyone outside the neighborhood, or days when both parents and kids are out of work and school.

Think about how you'll fill your time without your kids' favorite music CDs or favorite websites. Maybe you use the time to plant some trees, enjoy Boggle or Clue, or go through years of photographs. Consider having everyone in the family read an age-appropriate book about life in a simpler era. We love the *Little House on the Prairie* series (ages 8–12) by Laura Ingalls Wilder.

For the adults, a book we adore is *See You Next Century* by Ward Logan. It's a fascinating account of a young New York family that checks out of the 21st century. You may not last much longer than a day or two, but this family held out for a year, eating only what they could grow, heating and cooking with wood, and getting around on a horse-drawn cart.

Encourage older children to keep notes of their thoughts and feelings during the experience (by hand, of course). After the techno time-out is over, talk about it. Ask each participant to identify one "takeaway"—the most meaningful part of the experiment for them. As a result of the experience, consider cutting back on your use of technology, especially if it will help you be more original, creative, or engaged in family life.

We 21st-century people have no better friend than technology. It lets us move through life more easily. And it adds amazing efficiencies like communicating with loved ones far away in real time, being able to see a photograph as soon as you've taken it or finding the perfect play group on line. But consider, even if for just twenty-four hours, letting your kids experience something very, very different—a quiet, beep-free existence without electronics. Truly a world of their own.

"In-House" Tech Support

Is your child a budding computer geek? Is there a pint-sized IT wannabe living in your house? Some kids seem to have a natural knack for technology, which often reveals itself at a very young age. As these digital kids get older, they can be incredibly helpful sourcing, setting up, and maintaining at-home electronics. Having someone in the family who's good at this is a blessing, especially when you look at the cost of hiring a computer person to come out or paying for questionable quality online tech support.

If your 'tween or teen is the one you turn to when the wireless network goes down or you've having trouble uploading photos, take this to the next level. Help develop your child's natural ability and, in the process, contribute significantly to the family and feel really good about it.

There are lots of ways to encourage this skill set. If you are comfortable paying your children for chores, establish a set fee (a "retainer" in grown-up business terms). Your child earns $5 or $10 a week for helping with all things technology, from DVRing a History Channel special for a younger sibling to helping you organize your online photos or stripping an old hard drive before donating a computer.

If you don't like the idea of giving your child money for duties, include tech tasks in your child's regular chore list. Goodness knows it's cooler to fix a broken router than fold socks. Help her learn more about computers and technology. If you're skilled in this area, take the time to share your knowledge and monitor your daughter as she tackles increasingly complicated projects. If techno isn't your thing, guide your child to useful websites (like DIY-computer repair.com, or Doityourself.com) to hone her skills.

Got a friend or neighbor who works in the IT or high-tech field? Perhaps your teen could spend some time with this person while he or she tinkers at home or even at a workplace. She'll learn some immediate lessons and see what the real world of IT is all about. Also check into free or low-cost computer camps or classes. City parks and libraries frequently offer these during school vacations. And, in some districts, after-school programs offer computer learning as an optional activity.

By putting your confidence in your child and acknowledging her budding expertise, you help her begin to see herself in a whole new light. And, who knows, a few years of around-the-house IT could turn into a part-time job or maybe even a career.

Try Before You Buy . . . or Not

Technology changes at a crazy pace. In no time, that state-of-the-art cell phone you've got will be a dinosaur worth a fraction of what you paid for it. Adults know these things, but it's hard to convince kids that some very cool digital gadget they're dying for may not be a really good idea at all. If your fifteen-year-old son has been diligently saving his baby-sitting money for a Wii game or a mini video camera, you can help him become a better consumer by encouraging him to swap for it before he pops for it.

Basically, find someone who has the thing you're considering buying. (This probably won't be difficult; if your teen wants it, a friend probably already has it.) Depending on your arrangement, you borrow the item for a day or two or more, and pre-arrange when the equipment will be returned to its owner. The idea works just as well for adult toys and gadgets like cameras or a mini laptop.

It's a simple idea, but because it involves potentially valuable electronics and other people's children, you need to be careful with whom you swap. We've tried it with close friends and relatives—the kinds of parents who encourage their kids to be exceedingly careful with other people's things. You need to have confidence that the family with which you're swapping is comfortable with the idea, and you have to be confident that you'll return their goods in the same shape you borrowed them. That means monitoring your children and being accountable.

What's interesting about this is that, at least in our experience, trying out the product sometimes convinces us, or that eager teen, that it's not all that great. A case in point was a friend's smoothie maker. What a wonderful gadget, we thought. It will encourage us to eat more fresh fruit, even on hurried mornings. We tried our friend's fancy machine for a couple of days and enjoyed whipping up quite a few yummy smoothies.

But as the chopping and whirring went on, we realized that the maker was really no different from the blender that had been stashed in the attic for years. Sure, the blender was old, and we had to make sure the fruit was cut up fairly small, but it worked just fine. And yes, we did make and eat lots of blender smoothies that summer and beyond.

You can take this idea to the next level when you agree with neighbors to share seldom-used electronic or other types of equipment. Again, you need to have a trusting and easy relationship with someone if you're going to be borrowing their things. But sharing expensive equipment can be an absolutely brilliant way to save money.

Most people who do this start small, maybe with a portable DVD player or personal assistance device. Some communities are doing it on an organized level, but not, as we've heard, for electronics. (Here's a fun aside. We learned of one small town library that lets members check out cake pans in fun shapes like dinosaurs and hearts. The librarian started collecting them at garage sales, and people love the idea of being able to borrow something they'd never use more than once a year. A dinosaur birthday cake is a really neat thing to be able to produce; free pans make it even better.)

Sharing builds a sense of community, and it teaches respect for other people's property. Take a good look around your house—

couldn't you make do with half as many high-tech gadgets? We could! Check out Chapter 5 where we've got much more on swapping, bartering, and sharing.

CyberArts

Technology is a terrific way to encourage your child to discover her inner artist by experimenting with free online arts like filmmaking, clothing design, illustration, graphic design, and photography. When our friend Kris Cain's twins were six, they asked if she'd help them learn to make a movie. So she set them up with her old computer and taught them to use Windows Movie Maker. Okay, maybe you have to be the child of a technology and photography guru like Kris to use these applications at age six, but the point is, it is easy, fun, and free!

Windows Movie Maker software, introduced with Windows ME and now included in all Windows programs, lets you create and edit your own video movies. Users import still and moving pictures they've taken or found into the program. The next step is to edit and manipulate the images, adding special effects and even audio tracks. Newer versions (like Windows Live Movie Maker) can even capture high-definition content. If you are a "Mac" rather than a "PC" family, iMovie offers comparable movie-making software.

Very cool fun. Making a movie offers all kinds of skill-building and lets kids experiment with an exciting, creative medium. If your kids don't love this free and engaging activity, you certainly will.

Budding fashionistas and parents of same, listen up. The web is full of online places to indulge your passion for fashion. One of them is fashionfantasygame.com, a site for 'tweens and teens. Players assume the role of designer or store owner. The designers produce fashions and get them to market. And shop owners "rent" a virtual retail store, stock their shelves from endless choices, and figure out how to attract customers. Both designers and owners must watch their expenses and budget wisely.

Also, there are lots of "makeover" games in which makeup and clothing "experts" can give famous and not-so-famous people a whole new look. Like any website, you'll want to search and vet these sites before approving them for your child.

The website Kinderart.com is exciting and diverse. As on many sites, you'll also find pop-up ads and plenty of things you can buy. But the best content is free, like individualized lessons you can print out and use to build abilities in drawing, architecture, drama, and folk art. The Children's Museum of Indianapolis (recognized as one of the world's best children's museums) runs a great website with age-appropriate activities and fun ways to experience art and lots of other subjects. You'll find it at childrensmuseum.org.

If you've got kids who want to learn to play guitar, draw still art, sing opera, or throw pots, an easy resource for how-to's and demonstrations is YouTube.com. Here, again, you'll have to do some research and put in some time to make sure the videos are appropriate and instructive. But the possibilities are absolutely endless. YouTube is also a super choice for introducing your children to an artist or dance form.

Mini musicians, or not-so-talented kids who just love music, are well served by a site called Children's Music Web (childrensmusic.org). The ad-free site helps youngsters do everything from creating their own radio station to making a webcast. Younger kids can sing along with favorite songs.

Speaking of the little ones—who may not be ready for some of the hands-on learning activities—you can always spend some quality time with them on the Crayola.com site. You'll find games, coloring pages to print, and certificate- and card-making. It's a solid, safe site you'll want to come back to.

Reach Out (into Cyberspace) and Touch

The Internet has changed our lives in many ways. One great plus is the ease with which we can connect with others, including helping those in need. Reaching out online is a wonderful way to teach values while strengthening your family *and* your ties with the community.

It's the little things

Teach your children to think of others every day in simple ways. We love Mercy Corps and its family of click-to-give sites. If you start at HungerSite.org, it takes two minutes to visit each of their several deserving sites. With each click, sponsors give food, provide mammograms, protect the rainforest, and assist animals in need. It's safe and reliable, and it's a wonderful way to make a daily difference.

Build community

As a family, come up with a neighborhood project, and create and roll out a campaign. The theme can be whatever moves your crew—recycling, shoveling snow for elderly neighbors, cleaning up a local park, or holding a fundraiser for a special cause.

Come up with a list of what needs to happen and when, everything from publicizing the effort through e-mail or a neighborhood website, to getting volunteers, thanking them for their effort, and assessing how well it went. They'll want to write and illustrate a flyer, and maybe even create a simple spreadsheet to track activity, like the schedule for watering and weeding Mrs. Brown's lawn. A neighborhood project can be demanding, and it will definitely require commitment and involvement. Get other families involved, including those with parents whose skills complement your own.

Pal around

Okay, writing to kids across the world requires a keyboard, not a pen, these days, but the pen pal idea is alive and well. A number of websites offer kids the opportunity to become e-mail buddies with kids in other states and countries. Because they come and go fairly often, we haven't listed them here. Instead, we suggest you do a search for "safe pen pal sites for kids" and get started that way. You may also want to help your child become a pen pal with the son or daughter of a member of the military.

You'll find sites for this as well but, as always, vet them carefully before letting your children sign on. Review these sites thoroughly to be sure they aren't really promoting online dating. A not-for-profit organization (usually indicated by .org) is often a safer starting point. Also, you should not have to pay for a pen pal, so be careful of sites that charge.

Bookmark a few good outreach sites you can turn to when the kids are bored and need a reminder of just how fortunate they are.

- **HELPOTHERS.ORG** is filled with excellent tactics for lending a hand. You can send in your own kindness story to inspire others with your good deed.
- **NETWORKFORGOOD.ORG** has information about kids' giving, virtual volunteering, and lots of ways to reach out and help.

- **SMALLACT.COM** is a fascinating site that asks people to make it their home page. In exchange, advertisers donate a penny per day. Registrants choose the charity of their choice. The site also seeks to inspire a minute of kindness per day per person. It doesn't sound like much, but when you do the math, the possibilities are world-changing.

If you are religiously affiliated, your denomination or place of worship may have online opportunities as well. Reaching out online has its detractors. Some people say it's a lazy person's way of helping someone else. We respectfully disagree. We've seen a tremendous amount of good accomplished online. For some people, especially those with mobility or time constraints, it can be a substitute for getting out in person. For others, it may represent a small daily act of caring that's supplemented with mentoring, building, or writing checks to support good causes.

Our journey is coming to an end. But, then again, the journey called motherhood is never-ending. We hope we've helped you go beyond the essential eating, napping, and playing to get more out of the days you spend with your children—enjoyably, affordably, and satisfied that you're becoming the best mom you can. Never perfect, but always improving.

Before we leave you, we want to make sure we've provided you with ways to dig deeper into the topics we've touched on in the book, plus some we couldn't get to but think you might want to know about. We hope you'll spend some time with Chapter 10's Resources and Freesources, and share them with others who care as much about smart, authentic parenting as you do.

Resources and
Freesources

S O WHERE DO YOU GO FROM HERE in your pursuit
of more meaningful, affordable experiences with your children?
If you're anything like us, you love the Internet for bringing a
world of information to your fingertips. But you also know you
have to be careful, not only about what your kids see and use, but
about the potential time- and money-wasting opportunities lurking
on the Internet for grown-ups, as well.

In this chapter, we share some of our best picks for online and
other resources that can take you beyond the pages in the chapters.
The idea is to give you tools to dig deeper, learn more, do more,
and save more.

We apologize in advance if a site or resource is no longer in existence or has changed its contact information since the book went
to press. The Internet's strength is that it is dynamic, but it can be

hard to keep up with the constant changes. Our aim has been to include solid sites that had been around for a while when we listed them or newer sites that appeared to have staying power.

Saving Money

- **UPROMISE.COM.** More than a million people use this resource. When you sign up, a portion of your everyday spending on things like groceries, restaurants, and online shopping accumulates to save for college. The earnings accrue until you decide to invest them in a 529 college savings plan, use them to pay off student loans, or for other related purposes. Users benefit by inviting others into the plan.

- **SAVINGADVICE.COM.** This site teaches people how to save money through even the smallest alterations to their lives. For example, spending a few dollars buying new air filters can save you hundreds in heating costs because your heating system doesn't have to work as hard. Tips, terms, and forums are included, too.

- **CLARKHOWARD.COM.** This is a content-rich site with free, reliable information and insights from consumer and financial guru Clark Howard. You'll find everything from charts that tell you how much you have to save to become a millionaire to the latest on work-from-home schemes, best investment products, credit card deals, saving for college, and buying a car. You can also view videos and notes from his popular radio show.

- **PENNYWISEGUIDES.COM.** PWG "is a collection of tips and tricks for saving money and spending smartly." Users share their tips and write succinct, downloadable guides on all kinds of topics, like how to save money on eyeglasses, and spend less on travel and feeding your baby.

- **SAVEMONEY.COM.** Save all over the place, including in the choices you make regarding education, housing, insurance, pets, shopping, and more. Registering gets you alerts, newsletters, and access to online forums.
- **CRAIGSLIST.COM.** Bottom line—there's an amazing amount of great, cheap stuff on Craigslist if you know what you're looking for, and how to read and interpret postings. Buy with caution to avoid scams. Buy smart, be aware of who you are purchasing from, and what you are buying.

Family and Home Life

- **SURFNETPARENTS.COM.** Click through to reveal a ton of content about family life. Sections address enjoying inside time, outside games for teens, pool safety, what to pack when you're flying, and fun ways to learn the ABCs. The site is for parents of babies to teens.
- **CREATIVEHOMEMAKING.COM.** Rachel Paxton offers a treasure trove of information about cooking, cleaning, gardening, and home organizing. There's a great recipe database, a weekly newsletter, and tips on how to find a qualified contractor, make a homemade facial mask, how to save money on gas, and good deals at big national retailers.
- **PBS.ORG/PARENT.** The Public Broadcasting System parents' website has a wealth of information on child development, health, and, of course, PBS listings.

Food and Nutrition

- **CHILDRENSRECIPES.COM.** This kid-friendly site allows children to find recipes that they would like to try. They can even post their own recipes.
- **COOKINGWITHKIDS.COM.** The name says it all—a fun, interactive site with recipes, cooking tips, and even educational food quizzes for engaging kids in the world of food and cooking.
- **SPATULATTA.COM.** Kids teach other kids how to cook through step-by-step videos. The site encourages healthy eating in the process.
- **FRUITSANDVEGGIESMOREMATTERS.ORG.** Great content about food, nutrition, and getting kids involved in buying, cooking, and eating good food. The site is produced by the Produce for Better Health Foundation.

Swapping and Sharing

- **FREECYCLE.COM.** This is a network of more than 4,000 groups made up of millions of people who are giving and getting stuff for free by bartering. The site has a strong green component because it's all about keeping those treasures somebody may want out of landfills.
- **WEBFLOSS.COM.** Amy Lynn's big, busy website offers great deals ("hand-picked for security") on printable retail and restaurant coupons, plus travel deals, kids-eat-free offers, and blog entries on thrift shopping and other ways to save. Check out the Getting Started Guide.
- **BOOKMOOCH.COM.** BookMooch is a community for exchanging used books. Give away books and get trading points in return that you use to "buy" books you want. You get more points for more

costly or rare books. There's no cost, other than for mailing the books. You can also benefit charities with your points.

- **MAINSTREETBARTER.COM.** Doug Dagenais is a nationally recognized barter expert. He's written a book that addresses strategies for saving cash by bartering. There is a fee to use this service, so look it over carefully.
- **ZWAGGLE.COM.** This is a national network of parents who come together to share. You receive Zwaggle points (known as zoints) by giving your gently used things to other families, then use zoints to obtain new things for your family. The site also offers a points-for-charity component.
- **WICKEDCOOLDEALS.COM.** This is a good blog about deals, offers, promotions, coupons, two-fers, and rebates. It's run by a mom who gets the whole savings thing.
- **TOTALLYFREESTUFF.COM.** Easy-to-use site with daily postings, a daily newsletter, and a good search tool. It's been around since 1998.

Recycling and the Environment

- **ECOCHIC.TOP-SITE-LIST.COM.** This site lists lots of eco-friendly websites for families and single moms.
- **EPA.GOV/RECYCLECITY.** This is an interactive site with activities for kids and parents to help them become more familiar with recycling. Includes green games and activities.
- **PBSKIDS.ORG/EEKOWORLD.** This PBS website teaches kids, ages six to nine, how they can help take care of the earth. Animated characters use games and activities to present facts about ecosystems and pollution.

- **NATURECHALLENGEFORKIDS.COM.** This David Suzuki Foundation website starts with ten simple ways you can protect nature, followed by four challenge activities that offer first-hand experiences with the natural world.
- **EARTHEASY.COM.** This site offers up to twenty kid-friendly websites that are appropriate for young learners interested in recycling. It's all about how to do what you do, including play, in a sustainable way.
- **HGTV.COM.** Find information on what makes a home green and various examples of environmentally friendly homes. Type "environment" into the search box.

Gardening with Kids

- **EDIBLESCHOOLYARD.ORG/GARDEN.** Alice Waters started the Edible Schoolyard concept in 1995 at a school in Berkeley, California. It's a way to help kids understand how food gets on their plate and why eating well matters. There are similar programs across the country.
- **WHOFARM.ORG.** Read the story of the White House Organic Farm project. The WHOfarm mobile is a couple of school buses fused together with a garden on top. You'll also learn about the White House kitchen garden started by First Lady Michelle Obama in 2009.
- **COLOSTATE.EDU.** Once inside the website, search for "gardening with children." You'll find excellent information provided by the University of Colorado Cooperative Extension specialists. There's similar content with a different twist from the University of New Hampshire at horticulture.unh.edu/ggg.html.

Parties and Celebrations

- **BIRTHDAYEXPRESS.COM.** This is a great resource for packaged parties you can purchase on a variety of themes if you're unable to or don't have time to do it yourself. There are supplies, activities, banners, table ware, activities, piñatas, and other party stuff. Check out their clearance section.
- **COOLEST-BIRTHDAY-CAKES.COM.** This site contains thousands of homemade birthday cakes "even amateurs can make." Themes include circus, zoo, sports, trucks, cars, trains, dolls, baby cakes, character cakes, and more. Get instructions, and get inspired.
- **EVITE.COM.** This site is probably familiar. You can create and send great-looking invitations for free and get other good party ideas.
- **MITZVAHMARKET.COM.** Sheri Lapidus and Erica Salmon have created an online resource for families planning Bar/Bat Mitzvahs. Even if you're not, they've got great ideas for all kinds of celebrations, including practical ideas for keeping costs in check and creative ideas for making parties more meaningful while also encouraging mitzvahs and good deeds.

School and Learning

- **SCORE-ED.COM.** Sharon Marshall Lockett is an education consultant with great ideas about helping kids learn. Check out her book, *Home Sweet Homework*, which is offered on the website.
- **THEORGANIZEDSTUDENT.COM.** This site will give you some good ideas about the hows and whys of student organization. Donna Goldberg is an expert in the field and has also written a good book, *The Organized Student*, which you can order from the site.

- **KEEPANDSHARE.COM, CALENDAR.GOOGLE.COM, COZI.COM.** Create free online calendars at these and similar sites to help keep kids organized during the school year.
- **ALIBRIS.COM.** Click on the "textbooks" tab and take it from there. You'll find a huge selection of textbooks for all levels. There are resources for home-schooling parents, as well.
- **FUNBRAIN.COM.** Widely used by parents and teachers, it offers interactive online learning games for children.
- **HALF.COM.** Look for their Textbook Superstore. Half.com is an eBay site.
- **AMAZON.COM/TEXTBOOKS.** The giant online retailer has a ton of new and used textbooks at discount prices. Shop around to make sure you're getting a deal.
- **MYSCHOOLHOUSE.COM.** This site offers lessons and worksheets for use at home or in the classroom.
- **ASKKIDS.COM.** Lots of activities for young, active learners in subject areas such as math, science, English, and history.
- **FREE.ED.GOV.** FREE stands for Federal Resources for Educational Excellence. The site has a wealth of educational materials produced by federal agencies. Great for home-schoolers and parents who want to enhance their child's education.
- **WEEKLYREADER.COM.** It's just like you had as a kid, but now updated with contests, giveaways, and current events–related stories for kids.
- **TIMEFORKIDS.COM.** This site contains articles and quizzes on current and historic issues.
- **COOLMATH.COM.** Find activities, challenges, and other ways to spark kids' interest and abilities in math.
- **WORDCENTRAL.COM.** This is Merriam-Webster's kid-friendly version of dictionary.com. It offers quizzes and word puzzles to enhance the learning of vocabulary.

Health and Wellness

- **KIDSHEALTH.ORG.** Keep kids healthier during the school year and all year long. This site is run by The Nemours Foundation, a non-profit organization dedicated to "improving the health and spirit of children." There's fun-to-explore content on feelings, how the body works, staying safe, health problems, and prevention.
- **CDC.GOV/FAMILY.** There's also good health content at this site run by the U.S. Centers for Disease Control and Prevention.
- **LOVETOKNOW.COM.** More good content about health and wellness (plus, plenty on fashion and entertainment, too!).

Technology

- **FUNBRAIN.COM.** Widely used by parents and teachers, it offers interactive online learning games for children.
- **SHUTTERFLY.COM, PHOTOBOOKMEMORIES.COM, PICABOO.COM.** These and other sites help you manage your digital photos, including making affordable albums and other cool stuff with photos. It's easier than ever to do this—all digital, no scissors required.
- **YOUTHLEARN.ORG.** This site offers teaching techniques, projects, and after-school ideas that focus on technology. Click on the section called "kids creations" from the right-hand menu to see what great technology projects kids are coming up with. They're inspirational!
- **GRANDCHILDCONNECTION.COM.** At this site, grandparents "learn" how to make video connections with their far-away grandchildren. There are activities, subscriptions, and gear to buy.
- **SKYPE.COM.** This is a less costly way to connect online with

grandchildren or anybody else. You may pay as little as a few dollars a month for the video service. The computer on the other end
has to be signed on for the service as well, and both must have
video cameras. (Most new computers have them installed.) Read
grandchildren a story, put on a puppet show, or sing songs
together in real time.

- **TECHMAMAS.TYPEPAD.COM.** This blog covers tech topics for moms—
everything from social networking to the latest Apple products.
- **ANITABORG.ORG.** Check out ways that women can get more
involved with technology at the website of the Anita Borg Institute.
- **TECH.BLORGE.COM.** For techies in the know, this site lists the top
40 tech news websites.

Motherhood and Parenting

- **FAMILYEDUCATION.COM.** This highly interactive website has articles, quizzes, and even "mom's coffee break" ideas.
- **PARENTING.IVILLAGE.COM.** You can really spend some time on this
site. Message boards, daily news, and advice from the experts are
all here. iVillage also features customized calendars, mom-to-mom
advice in weekly newsletters, videos, and photo galleries.
- **MORE4KIDS.INFO.** More4kids recommends other websites for
every possible parenting category, such as pregnancy, naptime,
toys, etc.
- **MOMFINDS.COM.** This site offers time-saving strategies and buys
for moms on the go.
- **BABYCENTER.COM.** There is tons of content here for moms and
those who want to be, including journals, photos, ovulation cal-
culators, activities, checklists, newsletters, parenting tools, deals,
and free stuff.

• **CFW.TUFTS.EDU.** Tufts University's WebGuide is a directory that describes and provides links to other sites containing child development research and practical advice. Topics are selected on the basis of parent recommendations.

Financial Literacy

• **MYMONEY.GOV.** This is a U.S. government site dedicated to teaching the basics of financial education. There's information from twenty federal agencies, as well as advice on buying a home, balancing your checkbook, and investing your 401k.

• **OWNYOURMONEY.COM.** Through her seminars and coaching, financial coach and CPA Belinda Fuchs helps "transform the way people think, feel, and act about money."

• **360FINANCIALLITERACY.ORG.** This site is filled with financial strategies, statistics, and ideas for all stages of life, particularly for women.

• **PRACTICALMONEYSKILLS.COM.** Learn more about credit, debt, and other financial topics.

• **ORANGEKIDS.COM.** This is home to Planet Orange, a program that helps kids from first to sixth grades learn about earning, spending, saving, and investing. It's sponsored by ING Direct, and offers a Parent Center and a Teacher Resource Center with lesson plans, curriculum information, and other tools.

• **MINT.COM.** This is a popular online personal finance system. The services are free, and include online money management and budgeting software. The site helps you see where you're spending money, how investments are performing, set up realistic budgets, and identify best financial deals.

• **SIMPLIFI.NET.** This is another free, money-management site that helps you develop and use a personal financial plan.

Childcare

- **CHILDCAREAWARE.ORG.** Child Care Aware, a program of the National Association of Child Care Resource & Referral Agencies (NACCRRA), offers advice for choosing the right provider and includes a search engine to help locate a babysitter.
- **BABYCENTER.COM.** Find articles on research and preparation required for locating a good daycare facility.
- **CARE.COM.** This site has a highly specific search engine to identify the type of help you need. It also offers free background checks.

Crafts and Activities

- **FAMILYFUNGO.COM.** Figure out what you want to do, and this site helps you do it. It contains lots of bright ideas about ways to connect with kids.
- **CRAFTIDEAS.INFO.** All types of craft ideas are offered here: seasonal, patriotic, felt, and clay.
- **CRAYOLA.COM/CRAFTS.** This is a well-respected site by the Crayola people. They've got a craft-of-the-day and other activity ideas. Head here on a rainy day; you won't be disappointed.
- **THEFAMILYCORNER.COM.** The Family Corner provides craft projects, kids' recipes, parenting advice, decorating ideas, frugal tips, and more.
- **DISCOVERYKIDS.COM.** This site contains fun and games related to animals and the environment.
- **KIDS.YAHOO.COM.** Yahoo offers a fun-filled site for kids, with lots of learning and interactive games.
- **SURFNETKIDS.COM.** This is an informative site of sites—see what else is out there on the Internet that could benefit your family.

- **JRRANGER.SOUTHCAROLINAPARKS.COM/GAMES**. The South Carolina Department of Parks, Recreation, and Tourism has good travel/boredom-busting games and activities. Grown-up sanity-saving tips, too.
- **PBS.ORG/KIDS**. Games, coloring, activities, stories, and more are featured in a kid-friendly format. It's from the people who bring you *Sesame Street, Mr. Rogers, Electric Company,* and *Caillou.*

Mommy Blogs

- **THENEWMOM.COM**. This has the range you'd expect—everything from the emotions of new motherhood to relevant books, tips, and support.
- **DIARYOFANEWMOM.BLOGSPOT.COM**. This is a trendy, fashionable site dedicated to issues that moms want to talk/hear about, like the best portable plane/car seat and great mom-and-baby music classes.
- **MOM-101.COM**. This funny site dishes about the latest toy flops and provides "cool mom picks" in its back-to-school guide.
- **SAVVYSASSYMOMS.COM**. This blog aims to help moms become practical and intelligent, as well as chic and stylish.
- **BUSYMOM.NET**. This is a quirky blog about new-mom parenting experiences.
- **RADICALPARENTING.COM**. This site lists the 50 "best" mom blogs.
- **MOMMASAID.NET**. Written by a mom of two boys who "talk to her through the bathroom door," this blog is filled with humor and validation, helpful resources, and unique sanity-saving ideas.

Coupons and Deals

- **DEALSEEKINGMOM.COM**. You'll find lists of great freebies and coupons here.
- **MOMMYSAVERS.COM**. This site offers savings ideas, hot deals, and bargains, as well as family-friendly budget tips. Links to giveaways and coupons are included.
- **COUPONMOM.COM**. A whole universe of coupons can be printed directly from the site.
- **COUPONIZER.COM**. The Couponizer is a for-sale product that helps you save time and money, and get your coupons organized. The site offers free tips and ideas for couponing.

Shopping on the Cheap

- **THEBUDGETFASHIONISTA.COM**. This site offers shopping information, updates, plus coupons and deals.
- **BEST-BUY-DEAL.COM**. This site offers great prices and deals.
- **OVERSTOCK.COM**. Overstock sells a huge variety of products in all categories at discounted prices.
- **SMARTBARGAINS.COM**. This is another general discount site, similar to Overstock.com, where you'll find deals on everything from clothing and MP3 players to diamond earrings.

Working and Working from Home

- **WOMENFORHIRE.COM**. Women for Hire is the go-to resource for women looking for a job. Through live events, best-selling books, online resources, and coaching services, Women for Hire guides women back into the workforce in a safe online environment.

- **DSWA.ORG.** DSWA is an alliance dedicated to the needs of the female direct seller. A membership fee is required, and they offer educational support, information, and assistance for people involved in direct sales or who might want to be.
- **DMA.ORG.** The Direct Marketing Association is one of the first computer-user groups in the country. It's a resource for both novice and professional users.
- **THEWISDOMJOURNAL.COM.** Discover some solid ideas to get moms started earning extra cash.
- **MOMAUDIENCE.COM.** Moms showcase their businesses, blogs, products, and other offerings for free. The site includes a weekly e-mail with listings to help moms connect professionally and socially.
- **WORKINGMOTHER.COM.** Brought to you by the people who produce *Working Mother* magazine, the site addresses work-life balance, sibling issues, blogs, health, and best companies to work for.
- **MONEYFROMHOME.COM.** This site advertises itself as "100% scam free." It lists hundreds of available jobs women can do from home. It's been around for more than a decade.
- **THE GIFTIONARY.COM.** This national gift guide has an affiliate program. It is free to register as an affiliate and you'll receive a custom code and link to share on your site. You'll earn money every time you successfully refer a paid, approved customer to get listed on the site.

Online Safety

- **KIDPOWER.ORG.** This site helps empower children to protect themselves on the Internet and elsewhere.

- **ONGUARDONLINE.GOV.** Includes tips for parents to use when discussing Internet use for the first time with their kids.
- **CYBERBULLY411.ORG.** This self-empowering site allows children to learn what cyber-bullying is about, how they can prevent it, and how to respond if it happens to them or someone they know.

Neat Sites for Kids (with parent approval)

- **FIELDTRIPEARTH.COM.** Field Trip Earth is a resource for teachers, students, and people interested in wildlife conservation.
- **QUIZHUB.COM.** Your kids love trivia? Check out this academic quiz site for children in grades K–12.
- **CLASSBRAIN.COM.** This site tailors its information to different skill levels and ages. It makes learning fun.
- **NATIONALGEOGRAPHIC.COM.** This is an Internet classic. Click on the children's section to discover a world of fascinating information, plus quizzes, videos, and short stories from students around the world.
- **GIGGLEPOETRY.COM.** This cool site has hundreds of poems to read and rate. Kids can post their own poems, too.

Volunteering

- **VOLUNTEERMATCH.ORG.** Search by zip code for volunteer opportunities in your area. Interest areas include education, hunger, homelessness, and lots more.
- **NETWORKFORGOOD.ORG.** Learn more and make a difference at the Network for Good. Search for ways to give your time, read volunteers' personal stories, and learn about current crisis situations.

- **LIVEUNITED.ORG.** The website of The United Way is big, and packed with information and opportunity. You'll find tons of ways to get involved right in your own community.
- **AMERICASPROMISE.ORG.** Founded by General Colin Powell, the site is all about ways young people can make a difference mentoring, working with teens, and helping in classrooms and other settings.
- **HUNGERSITE.COM.** This is one of many sites on which sponsors give away products and services per visitor click. Visit daily to give free food and mammograms, help pets, and protect the environment.

Brick and Mortar—Non-virtual Resources

- **LIBRARIES.** There is a world of knowledge and growth within the walls of your local library. Become a regular.
- **PARKS.** Expand your horizons. Check out parks in different neighborhoods to mix things up. Hike, bike, picnic, relax with a book, discover historic sites, and more.
- **SCHOOLS.** Your local school playground (check the rules, as they vary) can be a wonderful place to take the kids to climb on equipment or kick a soccer ball around.
- **COLLEGES AND UNIVERSITIES.** If you're lucky enough to have higher education institutions in your community, take advantage. They are beautiful places to walk around and ride a bike. Many offer children's theater productions, film series, and live entertainment.
- **BOOKSTORES.** Some bookstores have wonderful inside play spaces for children and encourage them to come in. Some also have their own cafés. On a cold day, let the kids play and read for a while, then buy them a hot cocoa—quite a fun treat.

- **COMMUNITY CENTERS.** Your community probably has a center where adults and kids can play sports, swim, and participate in enrichment activities. Entrance may be free or nearly free.

Museums and Zoos

Check the websites or the paper to find special prices or free days.

Index

About the Authors

A woman of impressive literary and media accomplishments, **ROBYN SPIZMAN** is one of the leading how-to and inspirational voices in the gift-giving world. As a *New York Times* bestselling author, she is the founder of www.TheGiftionary.com, a gift guide from a to z featuring a galaxy of gifts. Robyn has written dozens of books and reports weekly on consumer topics, gifts, and giving. She has shared solid how-to tips for moms and creative gift-giving advice for almost three decades on many of America's leading talk shows, including repeated appearances on NBC's *Today Show*, MSNBC, CNN, *Home Matters*, The Discovery Channel, CNN Headline News, CNNfn, *Talk Back Live*, *Good Day New York*, *New York One*, CNBC and numerous ABC, NBC, CBS and Fox affiliates across the U.S.

Robyn has also been heard extensively on radio, from National Public Radio to *The Michael Jackson Show*. She has been featured in print media including: *The New York Times, USA Today, USA Weekend, Woman's Day, Ladies' Home Journal, Family Circle, Redbook, Cosmopolitan, Delta Sky Magazine, Dr. Laura's Perspective, Cosmo Girl, Parents Magazine, Better Homes & Gardens, Entrepreneur, Southern Living* and *Parade Magazine* among others.

Robyn has been a featured guest reporter on topics on the hottest gifts, products and toys in the country. As a consumer advocate, she appeared on Atlanta NBC Affiliate WXIA-TV for almost 30 years with her popular *Been There Bought That* segment. Robyn is a trendsetter in showcasing products of value. Since 2005, Robyn has hosted the Atlanta based hit show *The Giftionary* with Cindy & Ray on Star 94 - WSTR, the leading Top 40 Radio Station and a daily webpage on gifts at www.Star94.com. Seen on talk shows nationwide, she has helped hundreds of thousands of viewers save resources and give wisely.

A dedicated volunteer, Spizman serves on the advisory council of the Make-A-Wish Foundation, as shopping ambassador for Camp Twink Lakes and the foundation advisory council of eWomenNetwork, the largest online community of professional women, and was named one of the leading women in business by *Business to Business* magazine. Visit the author at www.robynspizman.com and www.TheGiftionary.com. Follow Robyn on twitter at www.twitter.com/TheGiftionary.

 **EVELYN SACKS** is a born communicator who parlayed an early ability to write and speak clearly into a successful thirty-five-year career. The ghost writer of four works of nonfiction, she is an accomplished lifestyle and business writer who has worked for leading companies including Kimberly-Clark, Coca-Cola, and Pfizer. Whether she is writing on wellness, assisting a celebrity with an autobiographical memoir or crafting a speech for a Fortune 500 CEO, the goal is clean, convincing communication. She and Robyn Spizman have collaborated on a number of projects and enjoy sharing one another's gifts and talents.